Swedenborg

ALSO BY GARY LACHMAN

Turn Off Your Mind: The Mystic Sixties and the Dark Side of the Age of Aquarius

A Secret History of Consciousness

A Dark Muse: A History of the Occult

In Search of P. D. Ouspensky: The Genius in the Shadow of Gurdjieff

The Dedalus Occult Reader: The Garden of Hermetic Dreams

Rudolf Steiner: An Introduction to His Life and Work

Politics and the Occult: The Left, the Right, and the Radically Unseen

The Dedalus Book of Literary Suicides: Dead Letters

Jung the Mystic: The Esoteric Dimensions of Carl Jung's Life and Teachings

The Quest for Hermes Trismegistus: From Ancient Egypt to the Modern World

WRITTEN AS GARY VALENTINE

New York Rocker: My Life in the Blank Generation with Blondie, Iggy Pop, and Others 1974–1981

Swedenborg:
An Introduction to His Life and Ideas

Gary Lachman

Jeremy P. Tarcher/Penguin
a member of
Penguin Group (USA) Inc.
New York

JEREMY P. TARCHER/PENGUIN
Published by the Penguin Group
Penguin Group (USA) Inc., 375 Hudson Street, New York, New York 10014, USA • Penguin Group (Canada), 90 Eglinton Avenue East, Suite 700, Toronto, Ontario M4P 2Y3, Canada (a division of Pearson Penguin Canada Inc.) • Penguin Books Ltd, 80 Strand, London WC2R 0RL, England • Penguin Ireland, 25 St Stephen's Green, Dublin 2, Ireland (a division of Penguin Books Ltd) • Penguin Group (Australia), 250 Camberwell Road, Camberwell, Victoria 3124, Australia (a division of Pearson Australia Group Pty Ltd) • Penguin Books India Pvt Ltd, 11 Community Centre, Panchsheel Park, New Delhi–110 017, India • Penguin Group (NZ), 67 Apollo Drive, Rosedale, North Shore 0632, New Zealand (a division of Pearson New Zealand Ltd) • Penguin Books (South Africa) (Pty) Ltd, 24 Sturdee Avenue, Rosebank, Johannesburg 2196, South Africa

Penguin Books Ltd, Registered Offices: 80 Strand, London WC2R 0RL, England

First Jeremy P. Tarcher edition 2012

Published simultaneously in Canada

Most Tarcher/Penguin books are available at special quantity discounts for bulk purchase for sales promotions, premiums, fund-raising, and educational needs. Special books or book excerpts also can be created to fit specific needs. For details, write Penguin Group (USA) Inc. Special Markets, 375 Hudson Street, New York, NY 10014.

ISBN 978-1-58542-938-7

Printed in the United States of America
10 9 8 7 6 5 4 3 2 1

Book design by Stephen McNeilly

Contents

Acknowledgments....vii
Swedenborg: Life and Works....ix
Introduction: The Scandinavian da Vinci....xiii

1 Northern Inventor....1
2 Soul Searching....37
3 The Night Sea Journey....71
4 Slayer of the Real....101

Endnotes....137
Select Bibliography of Swedenborg's Works....157
Index....169

Acknowledgments

I would like to thank Richard Lines, Stephen McNeilly and everyone at Swedenborg House for giving me such a warm welcome, as well as for suggesting the project and making their library available to me. I would also like to once again thank the British Library for its invaluable help. Special thanks to Mike Jay for his perceptive and stimulating remarks regarding schizophrenia and smell. And I am once again indebted to my sons Joshua and Max for their deep insights into all aspects of my work.

Swedenborg: Life and Works

1688—January 29, born Emanuel Swedberg.

1696—Emanuel's mother, Sara Behm, dies June 17.

1709—Emanuel graduates from Uppsala University.

1710—First trip abroad.

1714—Finishes designs of various inventions, including a water clock and submarine.

1716—Swedenborg publishes the first issues of the scientific journal *Daedalus Hyperboreus*.

1719—Family ennoblement and change of name to Swedenborg.

1723—Swedenborg's appointment as extraordinary assessor by the Board of Mines is recognized.

1734—Publishes the first part of his major philosophical and scientific work *The Principia*.

1735—Emanuel's father, Bishop Jesper Swedberg, dies.

1740–1—Publishes *The Economy of the Animal Kingdom*.

1743–4—First addressed by a spirit. Writes his *Journal of Dreams*.

1744–5—Publishes *The Animal Kingdom*.

1747—Resigns from Board of Mines.

1749–56—Publishes his major work *Arcana Caelestia*, a biblical exegesis in eight Latin volumes.

1757—Writes of a last judgment in the spirit world.

1758—While in London, Swedenborg publishes *Heaven and Hell*, *Worlds in Space*, *Last Judgment*, *New Jerusalem and Its Heavenly Doctrine* and *The White Horse*.

1763—Publishes *Divine Love and Wisdom*.

1764—Publishes *Divine Providence*.

1766—Publishes *The Apocalyspe Revealed*. Immanuel Kant publishes his attack on Swedenborg titled *Dreams of a Spirit Seer.*

1768—Publishes *Conjugial Love*.

1769—Publishes *The Interaction of the Soul and Body*.

1770—Swedenborg makes an appeal to King Adolf Frederic regarding the controversy in Sweden surrounding his *Conjugial Love*.

1771—Publishes *The True Christian Religion*. In the same year, he suffers a stroke but partially recovers.

1772—Writes to John Wesley. On Sunday, March 29, Swedenborg dies.

Introduction:
The Scandinavian da Vinci

Some years ago I approached a publisher with the idea of writing a book about the influence of the occult on Western literature. I had already published two books and several articles relating occultism and mysticism to popular culture and the history of ideas, and in writing these it became clear to me that what we call the occult has had a much greater impact on mainstream culture and our ideas about who we are than is generally assumed.[1] This struck me as an important insight, for it seemed to suggest that our ideas about the occult might need rethinking. Usually, for sensibilities fashioned by modern Western rationalism, anything concerning the occult is immediately rejected as absurd superstition, fit only for weak minds. On the other hand, for many people unhappy with the rationalist dispensation, anything concerning the occult is embraced unquestioningly—hence the devotees and true believers.

My own attitude toward the occult is, I think, somewhere in between these two extremes.[2] I am not an occultist, meaning I do not practice any particular occult art or discipline like astrology, tarot or alchemy, although, to be sure, many people today do. Yet, although I take much of what goes by the name occult with several grains of salt, I am not really a skeptic, at least not in the usual sense. Personal experience has convinced me that there are certain phenomena that cannot be explained by our usual rationalist assumptions; they are, however, nevertheless real. And my reading has made clear that throughout history, individuals of far greater intellect and mental powers than my own have accepted some aspects of occult thought. Moreover, our current view of reality, which accepts as real only that which can be measured, either by our senses or by devices designed to augment them, is relatively recent. It is only in the last few centuries that such a limited notion of what is real has held sway. Our "scientistic," materialistic view of reality is, historically speaking, embarrassingly provincial. I say "scientistic" rather than "scientific," because, while no enemy of science, I do regard the idea that modern materialist science can account for everything in the universe as exactly that, an *idea*—or, more accurately, an ideology, a belief. And although it is a belief held by many people, some of whom occupy positions of considerable power and authority in the world, it is, like other beliefs, no more a fact than they are. In many ways, it strikes me that our current view of the world is as superstitious and limiting as the kinds of beliefs the Enlightenment—the source of our current rationalist mind-set—supposedly liberated us from. And while I certainly do not accept ideas about the occult wholesale, I think that anyone who takes the time to view the material about it with an open mind, will see that rather than a grab bag of superstitions and muddled notions, it is really an indication of just how little we know about the world and ourselves.

The publisher I approached with the idea of a book on literature and the occult liked the idea and, after some discussion, commissioned me to write it. I was happy about this—not only for the very good reason that a writer always likes to get paid to write about what he is interested in, but also because, although I was familiar with much of the material, I would nevertheless have to go back and reread a great deal of it. This meant reacquainting myself with a lot of literature I had enjoyed reading the first time around, and going back to some I knew well. It also meant discovering writers and books that I had not yet encountered. In researching the book, several names were bound to turn up frequently and in different contexts—one of the things I enjoy most about writing books of this sort is discovering and tracing the connections between the sources of ideas and the people who were influenced by them. One name, however, seemed to turn up more than others. In many ways, it seemed that, no matter where I started, the trail I was following led more often than not to a single individual, whose importance for the history of Western esotericism—at least since the Enlightenment—can, I think, scarcely be exaggerated. That name was Emanuel Swedenborg. Finding Swedenborg practically everywhere in my reading, I was in a similar position to that of the angels that occupy his vision of heaven. No matter which way the angels turn, Swedenborg tells us, they always face

God. Though not as absolute as this, it did seem to me that whichever way my research went, there was Swedenborg.

Now, I was, of course, aware of Swedenborg before this. I had even written about him several years earlier for an excellent journal, dedicated to the "Western inner tradition," that, sadly, is no longer with us, *Gnosis*. That article was noticed by a Swedenborgian group, who asked if they could reprint it in their own journal, and it was later reprinted in an anthology of articles taken from the pages of *Gnosis*.[3] I had also read about Swedenborg before in several histories of the occult or the paranormal, mostly accounts of his clairvoyance and precognition, and his visits to the spirit world, so I certainly was not entirely surprised to find Swedenborg at the source of so much of what we can call "modern" occultism or esotericism. (I should say here that I am aware that many people who are better acquainted with Swedenborg's theological ideas than I am are eager to minimize the idea that he is a figure associated with the occult. They see this as a stigma, something that obscures his true importance and prevents him from getting the kind of serious scholarly attention he deserves. I can understand this, yet I have to say that trying to present an "occult-free" Swedenborg would, I think, have the opposite effect, and leave him where for many he is today, in the world of eccentric Christian sects, somewhere in the vicinity of the Jehovah's Witnesses.) It is unfortunate that the occult is a term overloaded with excessive and off-putting baggage, but if Swedenborg is to be associated with it, he is in good company. Respected figures like C. G. Jung, W. B. Yeats, and R. W. Emerson—all of whom were readers of Swedenborg—have been tarred with the same brush. I should also point out that J. W. Goethe, Edgar Allan Poe, August Strindberg, Honoré de Balzac and Charles Baudelaire were all linked firmly to Swedenborg. For example, Baudelaire's poem "Correspondances," perhaps his most well known, in which he tells us that "Nature is a temple," and which more or less invented Symbolism, the most influential art movement of the nineteenth century, is a poetic rendering of one of Swedenborg's most important ideas. Swedenborg was not only a central figure in the Western esoteric tradition; he was also crucial to much of mainstream Western culture as well.

It may seem to some, already familiar with Swedenborg, that what I am saying here is no surprise. They may already be aware of Swedenborg's importance. They probably know that Swedenborg's ideas, as well as the accounts of his psychic powers, drew the attention of respected thinkers of his time, and one of the most important philosophers of the modern age, Immanuel Kant. To put this in perspective, this would be the equivalent, in the last century, of Albert Einstein devoting considerable thought to, say, Rudolf Steiner's readings of the Akashic Record, and making a public statement about it. (Incidentally, Steiner and Swedenborg have much in common, a point I will come back to later.) To be sure, Kant's report on Swedenborg, *Dreams of a Spirit Seer Illustrated by Dreams of Metaphysics*, was negative, although there is evidence that Kant later changed his mind about Swedenborg's powers.[4] What is important, however, is the fact that the reports of Swedenborg's clairvoyance were considered so significant that a figure of Kant's stature was moved to have something to say about it. There is also evidence to suggest that Kant was motivated, at least in part, to write his most influential work, the *Critique of Pure Reason*, through his reading of Swedenborg's gargantuan *Arcana Caelestia*. The essence of Kant's philosophical work centered on epistemology, the study of how we know what we know, and he came to the conclusion that, by his definition, we can have knowledge only of the sensory world, or what he called the *phenomena*, things as we perceive them. Of the *noumena*, or things-in-themselves, we can know nothing. For a mind turned in this way, Swedenborg's accounts of heaven, hell and the spirit world must seem sheer fantasy. Yet Swedenborg was convinced that he had been granted access to inner worlds, worlds not limited to the sensory realm which Kant would argue were the sole source of human knowledge.[5] It was from these excursions into inner space that Swedenborg brought back, not only the "memorable relations" that depicted the character of the worlds beyond, but a metaphysics that transcended the limits of space and time, and put the human heart and mind at the center of reality.

In discovering Swedenborg at the source of so much of the modern Western esoteric tradition, I felt more and more that he was a figure I should definitely know more about. Like other esoteric thinkers, Swedenborg's writings are not an easy read. Swedenborg also has the added difficulty of having written in Latin, and in a time when the Bible commanded a central place in the minds of his audience that, for better or worse, it no longer enjoys. Probably more than anything else, the fact that his magnum opus, *Arcana Caelestia*, is devoted to an esoteric reading of the books of Genesis and Exodus, is the reason why Swedenborg's work still remains very much a kind of open secret—open because it is available to anyone who cares to look at it, secret because not many are inclined to do so. Esoteric readings of biblical texts are not uncommon in the occult tradition: the Jewish mystical school of Kabbalah is just that. Yet for people familiar with the esoteric tradition, but who would like to know more about Swedenborg, coming across these volumes can be an intimidating experience. The literary critic and philosopher George Steiner has bemoaned the fact that today we live in a kind of post-culture, a time when the religious and cultural landmarks that an earlier age knew well are unrecognized. We are, according to Steiner, rapidly becoming a generation without history. This is perhaps inevitable in a time, like ours, enjoying (if that is the correct word for it) swift and repeated technological change. Yet it certainly places some distance between ourselves and Swedenborg. The literate of his time knew their Bible and recognized the significance of understanding its "true" meaning. In many ways, people of a spiritual bent today are more familiar with exotic imports like Tibetan Buddhism or indigenous Indian Shamanism than they are with the spiritual traditions of the West. This is not to suggest that we should abandon our interest in these non-Western traditions, but like anything else, the spiritual pluralism of our time offers advantages and disadvantages. It is obvious, I think, that knowing the Bible is not as important today as it was a century ago, let alone in Swedenborg's time. And in any case, Swedenborg himself was selective about which parts of the Bible carried a higher, spiritual meaning.

Another reason why Swedenborg is not as well known as he should be is his sheer versatility.[6] Not only was Swedenborg the author of several immense tomes dealing with his esoteric reading of the Bible, his own spiritual experiences and insights, and a metaphysics of higher worlds; prior to the profound psychological crisis he experienced in his mid-fifties, Swedenborg was one of the most respected scientists of his era. He wrote on an astonishing number of subjects ranging from cosmology to the brain, and in many cases, his ideas and insights anticipated discoveries made only in our time. Along with this, Swedenborg was an inventor, a kind of Scandinavian da Vinci. Among his projected inventions were plans for a submarine, an aircraft and several other practical machines designed to improve production in the mining industry, to which he was financially and professionally linked. Along with his scientific and engineering interests, Swedenborg was for many years an Assessor of Swedish Mines, and his family, who were wealthy members of the social elite, owned shares in Sweden's most profitable mine. As part of this social elite, Swedenborg was also a statesman, and he contributed important papers on economics and drinking laws to the Swedish Parliament.[7] To improve his knowledge of engineering, and of the then young discipline of science in general, Swedenborg undertook many travels across Europe, staying for extended periods in London, Paris and other European cities. London was a favorite place for Swedenborg, and it was the site of some very crucial turning points in his life. He spent his last days there, living in humble surroundings, and in 1745, while physically in London, his spirit was taken on its first journey to the inner worlds.

So there is Swedenborg the spiritual thinker, Swedenborg the biblical scholar, Swedenborg the psychic, Swedenborg the scientist, Swedenborg the inventor, Swedenborg the statesman, Swedenborg the theologian and Swedenborg the traveler. If we recall that in his early career, it was assumed he would make a name for himself as a poet, there is also Swedenborg the poet. In our own time of specialization, such a polymathic career is a bit dizzying and, unfortunately, suspect. We tend to think that if someone has as many fingers as this in as many pies, he cannot be an expert in any of them, and ours, again unfortunately, is an era of the expert. This is true not only of academic readers: popular readers, too, want a simple image, an easy tag they can grab hold of; hence the decline in writers of the quality of, say, an Aldous Huxley, who was no expert (or, conversely, a multiple expert) yet who could write eloquently on a number of subjects. So Swedenborg's own prolific creativity may work against him.

And if the many hats I have already mentioned in Swedenborg's creative wardrobe were not enough to confuse our less than capacious minds, there is reason to suspect that a case can be made for one more: Swedenborg the secret agent. According to the research of Marsha Keith Schuchard, Swedenborg's many travels were not solely for the benefit of his scientific knowledge, nor for the profit of Sweden's mining industry. In several fascinating articles, Schuchard argues that Swedenborg was involved in a secret Swedish-French-Masonic plot to overthrow the then Hanoverian English monarchy, and to restore the Stuarts.[8] Readers fond of *The Da Vinci Code* and similar conspiracy theories will appreciate Schuchard's conclusions, which place Swedenborg at the center of a complicated network of secret alliances, involving the Young Pretender, the Knights Templar, Louis XV, the Freemasons and a Kabbalist or two. Along with the political intrigue, Schuchard's research also places Swedenborg in suggestively close contact with an individual who played a very important role in the transmission of occult and esoteric thought in Swedenborg's time, and who might have introduced both Swedenborg and a younger, more notorious contemporary to the Rosicrucian and Kabbalist sciences. The younger contemporary was the "magician" Giuseppe Balsamo, better known as Cagliostro. Given that Cagliostro acquired a reputation as a charlatan and mountebank and that, aside from his notoriety as a traveling magus, spreading the benefits of his Egyptian Masonry to the capitals of Europe, he has the distinction of being the last man imprisoned by the Inquisition, dying in the San Remo prison, it is understandable that followers of Swedenborg would want to dismiss any suggestion of contact between the two. Yet Schuchard's research makes a meeting possible, and argues strongly that the picture of Swedenborg, sanitized of any occult taint, is untenable. In Swedenborg's time, the occult sciences were just that, *sciences*, and were of deep interest not to frauds and fakes, but to the most incisive minds of the age, one of whom was Isaac Newton, who wrote much more about the "true" meaning of the Bible and alchemy than about the occult force for which he is most remembered, gravity. (If occult means unseen, then surely gravity is as occult as anything else we can think of.) In his early travels, Swedenborg wanted to meet Newton; it is doubtful that he did, but it is an indication of both the occult's once respectable appeal, and the centrality of the need to arrive at an unambiguous reading of the Bible, that both Swedenborg and the father of modern science should devote much of their life's work to this undertaking.[9]

With so many Swedenborgs, so many ways to approach him, and so many works from his own hand, it is understandable that the average reader interested in knowing more about him would find it difficult to know where to begin. And from the perspective of writing about him, to do Swedenborg justice would require a book as massive as one of his own. Thankfully, others have taken on this daunting task.[10] Here I intend to do something less challenging. I am not a Swedenborgian scholar, nor even a Swedenborgian. I come to Swedenborg from a background in the occult tradition of the West, and, more broadly, with an interest in what we can call "the history of consciousness." What I find of interest and importance in Swedenborg is limited by this perspective: yet my bias, I think, can supply a certain focus. What I would like to do here is simply to write about what I find interesting in this major, yet, for the most part, little-known Western thinker. A great deal will be left out: readers for whom Swedenborg's importance in the theological battles of the West is paramount will no doubt find little of value here. Others, who are curious about his place in Swedish history and politics, will also have to look elsewhere.[11] For other readers, it is possible that the brief account that follows may prompt them to dig a little deeper into the life and work of this still too-little-known figure, and to take a few steps of their own on their way to discovering Swedenborg.

Chapter One: Northern Inventor

1

Conveniently, Swedenborg's life can be broken down into two halves. The first half covers his childhood, his early travels and his career as a scientist until 1744, his fifty-sixth year. The second half is almost entirely devoted to the mission he believed he had been entrusted with during the crises he experienced in the years 1744–5. That mission was to communicate the true meaning of Scripture. By then Swedenborg had abandoned his scientific work. Until his spiritual crisis Swedenborg believed that it was through his work in science, either via one of his discoveries or theories, or through one of his inventions, that he would achieve fame, perhaps even that alluring will-o'-the-wisp, immortality. With the events of 1744–5, however, all that was thrown away, and his aching hunger for recognition—as well as his predilection for women—was seen in a new light. In *The Spiritual Diary*, a journal Swedenborg kept from 1746 to 1765 and probably the most in-depth and continuous record of "inner experience" we have, he is at pains to amend his past life.[1] In the early entries, Swedenborg often refers to himself as a sinner. In his *Journal of Dreams* (a document that precedes *The Spiritual Diary* and records the curious dreams and half-dream states that presaged Swedenborg's "conversion," if such we can call it), he is even more critical of himself. He writes that "it is best every hour and moment to confess oneself guilty of hell punishment," and that "a man ought always to confess himself guilty of numerous sins."[2]

Fairly heavy material, but we have to remember that Swedenborg was going through something more troubling than an average mid-life crisis. In characterizing a stage in psychological and spiritual growth, the psychologist C. G. Jung adopted an ancient Greek term, *enantiodromia*. This indicates a condition in which something turns into its opposite, a phenomenon that Jung was familiar with from his readings in alchemy, in which the reconciliation of opposites (male and female, light and dark) is a central theme. More than halfway through his life, Swedenborg went through what seems like a classic *enantiodromia*, in which his once good opinion of himself was radically altered. We can get a good idea of his state of mind during this difficult time in this remark about himself: "I, in spiritual things, am a stinking corpse."[3]

For many readers, this kind of self-recrimination and spiritual *mea culpa* might be off-putting; it appears to indulge in the very egotism that Swedenborg is eager to castigate. Sin is no longer a word in most of our vocabularies: we associate it with an old-fashioned and obsolete form of "fire and brimstone" religion, notwithstanding, however, that in today's uncertain climate such kinds of religions appear to be enjoying a renewed appeal. Today we are more tolerant of day-to-day improprieties, recognizing that we are only human, and where spirituality has taken the place of religion, we are more apt to see Swedenborg's hunger for fame as a sin, focusing as it does on the ego, than we would his appreciation of sex, a robust interest in which is part of our current recipe for health and well-being. In reading the entries in the *Journal of Dreams* which include Swedenborg's many self-criticisms, I found them disturbing. At times I found it difficult to continue and often had to put the book down. Yet we need to remember again that in Swedenborg's time, although its dominance was beginning to fade, religion and our relationship to God was still the most important thing in a person's life. We also need to realize that the experiences Swedenborg went through during his crisis were harrowing, and ran the gauntlet from extreme psychological dread to almost painful ecstasy. The aim of all esoteric practice is some form of rebirth, and in preparation for this, the neophyte must shed his old self: generally not a pleasant experience. The source of Swedenborg's initiation was, for him, the Lord; of this he had no doubts. One can imagine, then, that in contrast to the spiritual reality he was encountering, practically anyone's earthly life would have seemed to have "missed the mark," which is the original meaning of sin.

To get to that point, however, it took Swedenborg more than half a century, and while it is impossible to give a full account of that time here, it would be good to note some of the central facts.

*

Swedenborg was born Emanuel Swedberg on January 29, 1688, to a prosperous Stockholm family; he later changed his name to Swedenborg in 1719 when his family was ennobled. He was the third of nine children born to Emanuel's father, Jesper Swedberg—a regimental chaplain, who would later be appointed a pastor, a professor of theology at Uppsala (where the family moved when Swedenborg was two), and eventually a bishop—and Sara Behm, daughter of an official in the Swedish Board of Mines, and, incidentally, a wealthy mine owner. Accounts of Jesper Swedberg's character differ. According to one biographer, Signe Toksvig, "If ever a man rejoiced in himself and in all his works, that man was . . . Jesper Swedberg."[4] Toksvig found Jesper Swedberg self-righteous, self-occupied and self-deceived.[5] Yet for Lars Bergquist, Jesper was "one of the truly great prelates in the short era when Sweden held a dominant political and military position in Northern Europe,"[6] and his religious orientation was one of "moving toward a life in agreement with the demands of the Gospels constantly, every hour of the day."[7] Having read both Toksvig and Bergquist, it is difficult not to come away feeling that they are talking about different people.[8] This dissonance, though, is understandable. Bergquist is sympathetic to Swedenborg's teachings and their importance, as can clearly be appreciated from his book. Toksvig was a writer with an interest in fairy tales and the paranormal, and is sympathetic but critical in her account of Swedenborg's life and work. My impression is that Bergquist felt Toksvig's view of Jesper was unbalanced and wanted to compensate for this.

One gets the impression from Toksvig's account that Jesper was a man who wore his piety on his sleeve, and was not at all reluctant to display it. He took his religion with an admirable seriousness and was, according to Toksvig, singularly lacking in any sense of humor or irony about himself, or, evidently, practically anything else. Although Jesper lived until Swedenborg's forty-seventh year, by which time Swedenborg had made a considerable scientific name for himself (albeit outside Sweden), his father showed little or no interest in his son's achievements, other than to remind him often that if he intended to stay in the Lord's good favor, there was no better model for this than his own father's unimpeachable life. The details of that life Jesper generously made available to his children by presenting them with copies of his autobiography, all 1,012 pages of it, folio size. It would provide them, he said, with some "needed instruction in how to pass well through this world." And to prove he showed no favoritism, he also deposited a copy with the library at Uppsala University, so that those "less envious" could also benefit by it.[9] Those anonymous ones, along with his children, would have in his life an example of one upon whom the grace of the Lord was bestowed deservedly.

Jesper explained that he was the best person to relate the meaning and significance of his life, since "no one knows me better than I do myself, especially since, by the Grace of God, I am very careful to see that self-love neither blinds nor seduces me."[10] Swedenborg's own remarks about his father were, Toksvig recounts, dutiful and unexceptional. Yet it is difficult not to see in Swedenborg's later pronouncements on hypocrisy and his insistence that in the spiritual world, one "cannot think one thing and say another," the effect of living in the *penumbra* of a personality so assured of its own qualifications for sitting at the right hand of the Lord. The central characteristic of the higher worlds, Swedenborg tells us, is that there, unlike on our earthly plane, no difference exists between the inner and outer man. As the old line goes, in heaven "what you see is what you get." As readers of Swedenborg already know, self-love, the personality trait Jesper Swedberg so assiduously avoided, is the source of our separation from the Divine.[11] How Swedenborg can write of this with a simplicity that is more convincing than any argument, while his father writes of it with a lack of self-knowledge that, by any standards, seems exceptional, is one of the great mysteries of familial relations.

Of Sara Behm, Swedenborg's mother, we know little, other than that she was rich, seemed to have accepted her husband's character traits with equanimity, and that she died at the age of thirty when Emanuel was eight years old. If this was not a sufficient trauma for a young boy, his older brother Albrecht, age twelve, followed Sara soon after. Jesper praised her sweetness, kindness and gentleness, and her portrait suggests that Emanuel took after her. A year after his first wife's death, Jesper remarried, once again to a wealthy woman named Sara. Emanuel was lucky in acquiring a stepmother, Sara Bergia, who was warm and loving and who, out of a newly acquired brood of seven children (she herself had none), picked him as her favorite.[12] In later years, when he was recording the remarkable experiences making up his *Spiritual Diary*, he referred to his "mothers," the two Saras, with affection.

Swedenborg seems to have had a happy childhood, and in a book of his last years, *Conjugial Love*, which tells of the delights of married life in heaven, he speaks of the joys of childhood in a way that suggests that his memories of his own were fond. Children, he tells us,

> are content with the tiny presents they are given. They have no worries about food and clothing, or about the future. They do not look to the world or want a lot from it. They love their parents, their nurses, their child companions, with whom they engage in innocent play. They allow themselves to be guided, they listen and obey.[13]

Swedenborg himself never married and never had children, although in his last years in London, while living as a boarder with a shopkeeper in Clerkenwell, he was a favorite of the children in the neighborhood. Childhood, too, for Swedenborg, is not limited to this world, and in his vision of heaven, children who have departed this life are given to angel women who, in their earthly life, had a great love of them. Because these women loved all children as if they were their own, these new arrivals are given to them, and the children who have been taken from their parents love their angelic mothers in the same way. One suspects that in this beautiful image, Swedenborg was showing some gratitude to the stepmother who, of the many new charges she inherited from Jesper Swedberg, bestowed on him an especial love.

Yet, although Swedenborg played with his siblings, he also seems to have had a few other friends, whom he was unable to share with his brothers and sisters. Like the poet William Blake, who was deeply influenced by Swedenborg, in his early years Swedenborg apparently had visions. His unseen playmates—unseen, that is, by others—spoke to him of many things, and when he repeated these to his parents, they were astounded that he spoke so confidently of things beyond his years. When asked who had told him these things, Swedenborg answered that he had heard them from the boys with whom he played in the family's garden house. His parents knew he had been alone and decided that angels must be speaking through him, a presage of the extraordinary communications to come.

*

Although he would not, as his father wished, follow Jesper in a career in the Church, Swedenborg nevertheless grew up with a sense of the seriousness of religion and of the importance of man's finding the proper relationship with God, something that would seem unavoidable given his home environment. Into the blissful life of "tiny presents" and "child companions" darker thoughts often emerged, and he seems, unlike other children, not to have simply parroted these pieties but to have taken them to heart. Much later in life, in a letter written to a friend, Swedenborg explained that "From my 4th to 10th year, I was constantly in thought about God, salvation, and man's spiritual suffering. Several times I disclosed things that amazed my father and mother, who thought that angels must be speaking through me."[14]

Whether it was angels or a precocious concern with the needs of the spirit, in his early years, Swedenborg developed a skill that he would put to great use throughout his life. During his morning and evening prayers, he had learned how to control his breath, so that it seemed that he was hardly breathing. What his parents may have thought of this is unknown, and it is likely that he did not speak of it. But the impetus for this practice seems to have been that, by controlling his breath until it was unnoticeable, he could keep his mind fixed on the essential thing, God. This later became an awareness of the intimate relation between breath and concentration, or, in physiological terms, the lungs and the brain. Swedenborg's childhood habit of slowing his breath and focusing his mind would grow into one of his many intuitions about the functioning of the body that would later be established by medical science. Swedenborg's "search for the soul," the scientific pursuit that occupied much of his life, led through the brain, and it was only almost incidental that he arrived at several insights that modern science has since discovered, one being the "coincidence of the motion of the brain with respiration."[15]

Regulated breathing, and the chemical changes in the brain accompanying it, has for centuries been a tested means of entering altered states of consciousness. Many children know this, and hyperventilation is a common, if crude and occasionally dangerous, pastime for adolescents. Less doubtful are the varieties of breath control or "inspired" breathing the aim of which is to allow the practitioner to enter spiritual states of mind, and one recalls that the word we use for being somehow touched by "higher powers," "inspired," is a metaphor for breath. Eastern yogis have employed breathing techniques as aids in achieving *Samadhi* for ages, and the practice is not entirely absent from Christian worship as well, specifically in the Eastern Orthodox Church. In *Heaven and Hell*, his sequel to *The Doors of Perception*, and a title that seems to be a reference to Swedenborg, Aldous Huxley writes that changes in the levels of carbon dioxide in the blood can result in alterations in consciousness that, while not as radical as those produced by substances like mescaline and LSD, are nevertheless significant. Huxley writes: "A mixture (completely non-toxic) of seven parts of oxygen and three of carbon dioxide produces, in those who inhale it, certain physical and psychological changes." One of these changes is "a marked enhancement of the ability to 'see things,' when the eyes are closed." Carbon dioxide

> transports the subject to the Other World at the antipodes of his everyday consciousness [. . .] Long suspensions of breath lead to a high concentration of carbon dioxide in the lungs and blood, and this increase in the concentration of CO_2 lowers the efficiency of the brain as a reducing valve and permits the entry into consciousness of experiences, visionary or mystical, from "out there."[16]

Many who are aware of Swedenborg's conversion from scientist to seer accept that the change was precipitous, happening more or less out of nowhere. Yet if we recognize that by his mid-fifties, Swedenborg had been practicing a form of breath control for half a century, it should not be surprising that he passed into a realm of experience Eastern holy men spend an equal number of years trying to attain.

One more thing while we are on the subject of breathing. Control of the breath was important for Swedenborg, not only for his spiritual work but also for his scientific efforts. Inhibited breathing helped concentration because, through it, the mind could limit the degree it was disturbed by sense impressions. The most obvious sense impression associated with breathing is that of smell, and Swedenborg argues that when we are concentrating intently, we breathe through the mouth. Whether this is true universally is arguable: personally I doubt it. Observing my own breathing when concentrating, I find that I continue to breathe through my nose, although, as Swedenborg suggests, the breath becomes softer, more shallow and more regular (I find breathing orally more of a distraction). One thing a reader of Swedenborg's accounts of the spiritual worlds soon recognizes is that the sense of smell is very active there. Odors are very much a part of the higher spheres, and there is, as Toksvig remarks, a kind of spiritual smell register. Evil spirits give off and appreciate foul odors, those of vomit, excrement, decaying food, corpses and other nauseous scents, while good spirits exude more wholesome aromas; one of the heavenly odors is that of freshly baked bread, others are of fruit, flowers and frankincense. Swedenborg himself seemed to have possessed an acute sense of smell, and was able to put it to some very practical uses, such as being able to tell whether a servant was lying or not: presumably, the servant's perspiration was the tip-off.[17] Ours is a primarily visual culture and our consciousness is associated more with sight than with any of our other senses. The sense of smell, however, is one of the oldest senses and it is linked to the oldest part of our brain, what is known as the limbic system: in Paul MacLean's model of the "triune brain," it originates in the "reptilian brain," which developed much earlier than the specifically mammalian and human parts.[18]

Smells are also associated with extreme psychic conditions: both schizophrenia and manic depression (bipolar syndrome) are associated with heightened olfactory sensitivity, as is extreme anxiety and temporal lobe epilepsy. The question of Swedenborg's sanity will be addressed later on; here I should just like to point out that an open-minded reader of Swedenborg's *Journal of Dreams* and *The Spiritual Diary* would not be guilty of prejudice were they to wonder about Swedenborg's mental condition during the experiences he relates. The visions of heaven, hell and the spirit world, the conversations with spirits and angels, and the other remarkable encounters are, on the face of it, not dissimilar to accounts of psychotic episodes, and the radical mood swings—in which Swedenborg shifts from being a sinful "stinking corpse" to the ecstasy of God's grace—seem not too distant from the extreme emotional fluctuations associated with bipolar syndrome. During the "aura" preceding a seizure, people suffering from temporal lobe epilepsy often hallucinate smells, and individuals experiencing acute states of anxiety are sensitive to slight shifts in their sensory surroundings. Intriguing as these suggestions may be, except for the period around his initial spiritual crises, there is little to suggest that Swedenborg was a particularly anxious person: quite the opposite, he gives the impression of being inordinately calm and composed. And while temporal lobe epilepsy has, in recent years, been pressed into service to account for the altered states of consciousness associated with mystics, the attacks of trembling and tremors that Swedenborg reports were limited to particular occasions early in his crises, and were not a common feature throughout his life, which, one suspects, would be the case if he were epileptic.

Another possibility to account for Swedenborg's peculiarity about breath and smell can be found in a fascinating book by the biologist and zoologist Lyall Watson. In *Jacobson's Organ*—which, incidentally, contains some interesting material on the relation of schizophrenia and smell[19]—Watson argues that the organ in question, a patch of chemically sensitive nerve endings in the oral cavities of many vertebrates (amphibians, lizards, snakes and some mammals) also exists in humans, although its presence in ourselves is still contested or ignored by mainstream science. The peculiarity of Jacobson's organ,[20] named after its discoverer, the Dane Ludwig Levin Jacobson, is that it can detect and react to chemical stimuli of which we are otherwise unaware. One such are pheromones, the chemical perfumes that trigger sexual attraction. Less immediately titillating is the possibility that information about our environment—which includes other people—that comes to us in "hunches," intuitions and other unaccountable feelings and moods, may very well have its source in the unacknowledged detector located in our noses. Watson suggests that much that we consider the work of ESP and other paranormal abilities, may really be our own Jacobson's organs doing their job. It is a fascinating suggestion, and when Swedenborg used his nose to detect a dishonest servant, it is possible that his own Jacobson's organ was at work. There is, however, a further factor to account for Swedenborg's sensitivity to smell. We need to remember that although today we turn our noses up—literally—at automobile exhaust, cigarette smoke and other offensive scents, the London, Amsterdam and Stockholm of Swedenborg's time were much smellier than they are today, and for a man with a heightened olfactory works, eighteenth-century canals, gutters and sewers would very likely offer a robust suggestion as to what a whiff of the hellish realms would be like.

*

Probably the most important event of Swedenborg's early years happened when he was fourteen. In 1702, Jesper Swedberg was made Bishop of Skara: this entailed his moving the next year with his wife and children to the episcopal residence of Brunsbo. Emanuel, however, did not accompany his father. At the age of eleven, Swedenborg was enrolled at Uppsala University, and it was deemed more important for him to stay there and to continue his studies. So it came about that he moved in with his older sister Anna and her husband, Erik Benzelius. Swedenborg lived with his sister and brother-in-law for seven years, during which time Benzelius became the boy's mentor. Their relationship was close: Swedenborg spoke of Benzelius as his "father and better than a brother." From all reports, Benzelius, who was the university librarian, later professor of theology and Archbishop of Uppsala, was a brilliant man, with a true vocation for teaching and a real interest in the young. It is clear that Benzelius turned Swedenborg's avid mind in the direction of science, but there is also a possibility that it was through his brother-in-law that Swedenborg had his first encounter with the hermetic tradition. Benzelius was a Hebraist, he had edited Philo Judaeus, and knew F. M. van Helmont, co-author with Knorr von Rosenroth of the *Kabbala Denudata* (*Kabbalah Unveiled*). Knowledge of Hebrew was highly prized among Benzelius's peers, not only because it was the language of the Old Testament: it was also the language in which the books of the Kabbalah, the Jewish mystical tradition which had become so much a part of Renaissance humanism, communicated the secrets of the Divine. Benzelius had also met the philosopher Gottfried Wilhelm von Leibniz, who, according to Marsha Keith Schuchard, had become a member of a secret Rosicrucian society in 1667. Years later, Swedenborg would try unsuccessfully to meet Leibniz himself. The Rosicrucians were an esoteric society dedicated to the hermetic arts of alchemy and healing, and notices announcing their existence in 1616 caused a stir in central Europe. Curiously, one of the most noted scientist-philosophers of the time, René Descartes, recognized with Newton as being one of the founding souls of modern science, was suspected of being a Rosicrucian. Descartes' "mechanical" philosophy was subjected to much heated debate during

Swedenborg's university days, and Benzelius was one of the strongest supporters of the Frenchman's ideal of free inquiry, regardless of its deviation from accepted truths, which at that time meant Aristotle and the Bible. Jesper Swedberg was, understandably, vehemently opposed to it, and for much of his student years, Swedenborg was torn between his growing love of science and duty to his father's beliefs.

Swedenborg's studies included mathematics, astronomy and medicine, as well as areas we would call the humanities: history, oratory, Latin, Greek, and the classics. The only subjects he seems not to have taken were theology and law. Swedenborg excelled at his classes and took to student life, joining debating societies: in later life, because of a stutter, he would always be unsure about speaking in public, a hesitation that decided him against following a career as a teacher. Swedenborg seems to have shown a considerable zeal in these university debates, a sign, perhaps, of the urgency and hunger for accomplishment and recognition that color his scientific years. His eagerness earned him a rebuff when, after participating in several disputations—as the debates were called—he offered to preside at the following one on natural law. The rector of the university rejected his offer, commenting that the privilege was unusual for one so young and that "such a novelty might lead to disorder."[21] Having already given ground to the radical ideas and methodology of Descartes, the authorities no doubt did not want to offer the new thinkers too much encouragement.

Another area in which Swedenborg sought to excel was Latin verse, a practice more or less expected of scholars and gentlemen. Poetry was in fact the pursuit in which Swedenborg first believed he would make his name, although his accomplishments in this realm seem never to have reached beyond average. Swedenborg the student also seems to have gone in for all the finery given to the young men of his class. Jesper Swedberg had once railed self-righteously against the practice of wearing wigs, but a possible portrait of Swedenborg at eighteen shows a slightly effeminate young man, with a gentle face and smile, sporting a well-powdered wig, and what we can see of his dress suggests an equal dash. He was known to wear a rapier and, in his later life, when invited to dine with aristocrats or the wealthy, Swedenborg often appeared with a sword with a curiously ornate hilt. From the portrait one also gets a sense of a young man determined to make his mark in the world.

The hermetic tradition touched Swedenborg in his university studies as well. The professor he chose to preside over his graduation thesis lectured, among other things, on Pythagoras, Plato and Plotinus, an important triumvirate in the esoteric canon. Along with much dry Lutheran theology, a mystical stream ran through the curriculum, and traces of the emanationist metaphysics of the Neoplatonists can be found in Swedenborg's scientific and spiritual writings. Briefly, this view pictured creation as an emanation from God or the Divine, and not, as the orthodox belief had it, as being formed out of nothing. The idea of a stream of influence running from the higher worlds to the earthly realm is a central theme in hermetic thought, and is summed up in the alchemical formula "as above, so below." The same idea will emerge later in Swedenborg's philosophy of correspondences. This, however, would not be for many years, and at this point in his career, Swedenborg was as far from mysticism as most scientists are today.

In 1709, when he was twenty-one, Swedenborg concluded his formal education with a spoken dissertation on the sayings of a slave, Publilius Syrus, who became a popular author of plays among the Romans. These aphorisms gave Swedenborg an opportunity to display his erudition, as he accompanied each one-liner with as many interpretations and commentaries as he could gather from his reading. Looking at some of these sayings, one wonders how much they may have influenced his later writings: the measured Latin, the nuggets of wisdom and psychological penetration are reminiscent of the spare, dry pronouncements on the nature of the spirit worlds that would fill books like *Heaven and Hell* and *Conjugial Love*. One in particular, "Feigned goodness in speech is worse than malice," articulated the concern with hypocrisy that would come to dominate his ethical views, and he called on his audience, which included his father, to "Let our lips be consonant with our minds." It was a theme that he would take with him well beyond the borders of the Europe he was about to explore.

*

Benzelius had advised Swedenborg that he should travel and study science outside Sweden. England, in particular, he said, was the place to go. Jesper Swedberg had no interest in science and was not eager to part with the funds to finance a long trip abroad. With his schooling finished, Emanuel had moved to his father's house in Brunsbo, but he found the place deadening. He kept busy, learning music, bookbinding—Swedenborg would always prove himself a quick study in "hands-on" disciplines—collecting anything of interest, ancient coins and bones. Mostly he made notes, the start of a practice that would last the rest of his life. He was eager to visit other lands, to meet with other scientists and to learn from them all he could. The question of what he should do for a career was still unanswered, but he would soon have to make a decision. He was fascinated by the work of Sweden's most famous scientist and inventor, Christopher Polhem, and believed that his destiny lay in following the path the great man had opened up. Jesper Swedberg had already used his connections to petition Polhem to apprentice his son, but although Polhem had recognized Emanuel's potential, he rejected the idea. Benzelius, however, was convinced it was the right thing for Emanuel, and he tried again, and was successful. The only problem was that Swedenborg was nowhere to be found. It was only some time later that they discovered he was in England.

Exactly how Swedenborg got a berth on the merchant ship that took him across the North Sea is unclear. The time was not the best for sea travel: the Swedish army under Charles XII had been defeated by the Russians at Poltava. The King had been captured in Turkey, and the Danes, recognizing a good opportunity, decided to invade and regain Skåne, a southern region of Sweden, taken from them by the Swedes in 1658. The Danish fleet skirted the Swedish coast, making any voyage dangerous. Although the Swedes defeated the

Danes at Helsingborg in February 1710, sea travel was still ill advised. Nevertheless, when Swedenborg heard that a merchant ship was going to chance the crossing, he jumped at it. The warnings of danger proved correct. No fewer than four times was the twenty-two-year-old Swedenborg's life put in jeopardy. They had nearly run aground on a sandbank in dense fog, privateers boarded the ship, and later, an English patrol ship, mistaking them for the privateers, fired on them. But the last incident proved the most distressing and made a deep impression. Just outside London, some Swedes boarded the ship and persuaded Swedenborg to accompany them to the city. But the plague had broken out in Sweden and the English had commanded everyone on board to remain there in quarantine for six weeks. By joining his countrymen, Swedenborg broke the quarantine, the penalty for which was hanging. He was caught, and barely escaped the noose: luckily, he was only subject to a severe warning. But the virtue of possessing a "clean bill of health"—an essential item in those days—stayed with him and would return in the context of a very different crisis many years ahead. In later life, Swedenborg seemed to have had a peculiar luck when traveling, and the captain of one ship was always glad when he was aboard: his presence practically guaranteed a good voyage.

It would take us beyond the limits of this essay to recount all of Swedenborg's travels. The Grand Tour was *de rigueur* for young men of his class, and although he enjoyed travel and took in the standard sights in cities like London, Paris, Amsterdam, Rome, Milan and Hamburg, Swedenborg's main interest in traveling was to meet and exchange ideas with other men of science, either for his own use, or later in his capacity as Assessor of Mines. London in particular would become an important place for him, and although unmistakably Swedish, Swedenborg became something of a Londoner. He lodged in the city on six occasions, for varying lengths of time, and spent his last days there. London was also the scene for his initial entry into the world of spirits, and for a peculiarly eerie vision in which he was advised by an angel "not to indulge the belly too much at table."[22] It was in London several years after Swedenborg's death that an artist named William Blake and his young wife, Catherine, attended a meeting of the London Theosophical Society,[23] convened in order to establish "the truths contained in the Theological Writings of the honorable Emanuel Swedenborg."[24] The New Church that was later to grow out of this conference would initially have its strongest gathering in England. And although there is no record of a meeting between Blake and Swedenborg, it would not have been impossible. As Alexander Gilchrist suggests in his *Life of William Blake*, Swedenborg was active until his last days, and a fifteen-year-old Blake, having already heard about Swedenborg from his brother James, could very well have passed him on the street during his trips to the East End. Later, Blake would move in circles that certainly included Swedenborgians, even people who had known him, like the artist Philip James de Loutherbourg, who painted his portrait.[25]

It was also in London that Swedenborg may have encountered a curious figure in the history of the esoteric tradition, hinted at in my Introduction. According to the research of Marsha Keith Schuchard, it was in London that Swedenborg came into contact with the Rabbi Samuel Jacob Hayyim Falk. Another of Falk's students was Cagliostro, who, on his visits to London, was a frequent guest of de Loutherbourg. Falk is a mysterious, enigmatic figure, and it may be that he is one of the "unknown superiors" to whom W. B. Yeats—in his reminiscences of his time as a member of the Hermetic Order of the Golden Dawn—refers when speaking of the Order's history. Falk seems to have been at the hub of esoteric life in London at the time Swedenborg made his later visits, in 1744, 1748, 1758, 1766, as well as during his last days there. Falk was at the center of a community that included Freemasons, Kabbalists, Rosicrucians, alchemists and also the followers of Count Zinzendorf, leader of the Moravian Brethren, the "Herrnhuters." The Moravians were pietists, and their central concern was the "intensification, subjectivization and spiritualization of the Christian's personal engagement." Their aim was "total worship, embracing the whole man,"[26] an ideal that would appeal to Swedenborg, determined as he was to avoid the hypocritical fideism of the "inner and outer man." During his stay in London in 1744, Swedenborg lodged with some Moravian brothers. And in 1745, he stayed for ten weeks in a tavern on Wellclose Square, where Rabbi Falk had a mansion. It was in this tavern that the angel advised him to eat less.

There was another aspect of the Moravians that would have interested Swedenborg. The Moravians borrowed some of their doctrines from the Kabbalah, as well as from the followers of Sabbatai Zevi, the "False Messiah." Part of the Sabbatian worship involved sex, and it is possible that the several erotic entries in Swedenborg's diaries reflect his awareness of and participation in Count Zinzendorf's Sabbatian-Kabbalistic rites.[27] Rabbi Falk had been born into a Sabbatian community in Galicia (Poland), where he became a *Ba'al Shem*, "Master of the Divine Name," a title given to a practicing Kabbalistic magician. Falk must have been a fairly successful adept, as he was almost burned for heresy. Banished from Westphalia, he traveled first to Holland; then, in 1742, he arrived in London. Here he set up an alchemical laboratory on London Bridge, and from his house in the East End, he ran an esoteric school. Although a bachelor and, presumably, celibate from the time of his crisis, sex was an important ingredient in Swedenborg's philosophy, and he had some very liberal ideas about it, such as advocating concubinage and pre- and extramarital relations in certain circumstances. In Swedenborg's heaven, men and women find their true partners, who are not always the ones they knew on earth, and their sexual life continues: in fact, it is supposed to get even better. Loving eroticism between man and wife is a significant element in Kabbalah, representing on the earthly plane the creative act of the Divine, and helping to reunite the male and female spiritual principles. Swedenborg was highly sexed, and this interest in women was later transformed into a deeper understanding and appreciation of the spirituality and metaphysics of the erotic. By the time of the proposed contact with Falk, Swedenborg would have been practicing his breathing exercises for years: he had also tried automatic writing, and, in his travels to Hamburg, Prague, Amsterdam and Rome, he had stayed with Jewish communities where he presumably encountered the Kabbalah. We should repeat that

Swedenborg's life's work was relating the true meaning of the Bible, a task that Kabbalists had been engaging in for centuries. Although there are only a few brief references to the Kabbalah in Swedenborg's entire literary output—written in the *Philosopher's Notebook*, a posthumously published manuscript—and he denied having read the hermetic and alchemical thinkers, like Jacob Boehme, it is not difficult to detect more than a trace of the esoteric current flowing from these sources.

All of this, however, was, like its subject, hidden. On the surface, Swedenborg's travels were motivated by his voracious quest for knowledge, as well as his desire for fame. Side by side with his "esoteric" studies, Swedenborg devoted himself to mathematics, mechanics and astronomy. In his travels to England and elsewhere, he tended to take rooms with craftsmen, and learned from them their trade: watchmaking, cabinetry, brass working, marble inlay. In London he became, like Thomas De Quincey, a "cormorant" of the library and the bookstall, reading Newton daily, and investing in a horde of scientific instruments: prisms; microscopes; scales; quadrants; camera obscura; and, a particularly prized item, an air pump. His letters to Benzelius, describing his studies and encounters, were read by the Collegium Curiosorum, "The Guild of the Curious," the first Swedish scientific society. The members of the learned society wrote back, asking him to make contact with well-known figures like John Flamsteed, the Astronomer Royal. He did. Later, Swedenborg's detailed and informative letters would help him to become the editor of the first Swedish scientific journal, *Daedalus Hyperboreus* [Northern Inventor].

It must have been a gratifying and heady experience for a young man, sure of his powers and hungry for their use, on his own in a strange land for the first time. It was also in London that he began what would become an almost lifelong pursuit: to win the prize offered by Greenwich Observatory to devise a method of establishing longitude at sea. The prize eventually went to the English inventor John Harrison, who produced the chronometer. After London he went to Oxford, where he met the astronomer Edmund Halley, discoverer of the comet. While in Oxford his old interest in poetry resurfaced, and for a time the idea of becoming renowned through his verse reemerged. Yet this was only a brief idyll, triggered by his visit to the Bodleian Library. He would soon return to science, and on his travels to Holland, Paris, Hamburg and other points over the years to come, he continued to absorb as much of the scientific knowledge available as possible.

*

Before we go on to discuss Swedenborg's scientific work, it would be a good idea to make clear certain things. To call Swedenborg a scientist requires, I think, some explanation. He was not a scientist in the way we think of one today. In fact, there really was no word "scientist" at that time; the term would really only come into general use in the nineteenth century. We have to remember that what we think of as science was, in Swedenborg's time, very young, and was really considered a branch of philosophy. We have seen that people like Isaac Newton could devote as much time and energy—even more—to deciphering the Bible as he could to more scientific pursuits. Swedenborg did not engage in experiments, poring over test tubes and charts. His scientific work really fell into two camps: one was focused on practical results, the other on bringing together the work of others. In one camp he was an inventor, somewhere between Leonardo da Vinci and Thomas Edison. In the other camp he was one of the great synthesizers, linking up the work of others, adding to this his own insights and intuitions, and through this, opening up new areas of inquiry. Again, like da Vinci, Swedenborg had a passionate interest in anatomy. Unlike da Vinci, however, he did not dissect his own corpses, but rather relied on the research of other men. Swedenborg's reasons for doing this may strike us as odd. He said that relying on his own work would tempt him into placing too great an importance on it, and any discovery he could make would too easily obscure flaws in his thinking, as well as blind him to the significance of others' contributions. Although he freely admits his desire for fame, and his eager ambition to be "of some use" to Sweden, the old nemesis, self-love, seems to have placed some restraints on Swedenborg's methodology.

To get some idea of the inventive side of Swedenborg's genius, consider these extracts from a list of some fourteen proposed machines he sent to his brother-in-law:

> —The construction of a ship which, with its one-man crew, could go under the sea, in any desired direction, and could inflict much injury on enemy ships.

—A novel construction of a siphon, whereby water can be driven from a river to higher places, in great abundance and in a short time.
—On constructions (locks) even in places where there is no flow of water, whereby a whole ship with its cargo can be raised to a given height in one or two hours.
—New machines for condensing and exhausting air by means of water; and concerning a new air pump worked by water and mercury without any siphon, which works better and easier than the ordinary pump.
—A new construction of air guns, a thousand of which can be exploded by means of one siphon at the same time.
—A universal musical instrument whereby the most inexperienced player can produce all kinds of melodies, these being found marked on paper and in notes.
—A water clock with water as the indicator which, by its flow, shows all the moveable bodies in the heavens and produces other ingenious effects.
—A mechanical carriage which shall contain all kinds of works moved by the going of horses.
—A flying carriage, or the possibility of staying in the air and of being carried through it.[28]

Here we have a submarine, an aqueduct, a kind of machine gun, an early version of a DIY home entertainment center, an automobile, an airplane, and other mechanical wonders. The Europe Swedenborg was intent on conquering was a Europe awakening to a new delight in mechanized marvels. In the eighteenth century, the Frenchman Jacques de Vaucanson was renowned for his flute-playing android and mechanical excreting duck. Perhaps most well known was the Austrian Wolfgang von Kempelen's celebrated mechanical chess-playing Turk, a kind of proto–Deep Blue, whose long and varied career, beginning in 1769, brought him—it—into contact with nineteenth-century luminaries like Edgar Allan Poe, Napoleon and Beethoven. Human automata of various sorts, reflecting the new, mechanical picture of human beings and the cosmos, were popular entertainments: for the aristocracy in private showings and for the less fortunate public at carnivals and fairs.[29] Other technological wonders proved popular as well. Philip James de Loutherbourg, painter of Swedenborg's portrait and acquaintance of William Blake, would become famous and prosperous through the many special lighting and sound effects he created for David Garrick's theater in Drury Lane. Although strict scientists today might look down on these entertainments as beneath them—keeping their eye on the scowls of their peers—Swedenborg and others of his time had no hesitation in applying their mechanical skills in order to astonish and astound. Likewise, although today most of us would not celebrate a scientist who devised a new form of "smart bomb" or other innovation in warfare, Swedenborg had no scruples about using his abilities to aid Sweden's military efforts. Although he later had reason to be critical of his country, he remained a patriot throughout his life and wanted to see a strong Sweden. A submarine that could sink enemy ships, an airplane that could scout territories and possibly strike targets, a thousand-barreled air gun: each of these could be put to effective use, and in a time when Sweden's position in Europe was shaky, each could have meant recognition for the man who invented them.

Sadly, none of these marvels got far beyond Swedenborg's vivid imagination. In a letter to his brother-in-law, Swedenborg bemoaned the fact that his father had mislaid all of the drawings and calculations for his machines. His father also showed little interest in Swedenborg's efforts to develop a lunar method of establishing longitude at sea. Jesper Swedberg really had no insight into his son's talents, and it was left to Benzelius to find a niche for the young genius.

After returning home from his five years abroad, Swedenborg set to work editing the first issue of *Daedalus Hyperboreus*; filled with technical articles and designs for inventions, it was a kind of *Popular Mechanics* of its day. Most of the material related to the work of Sweden's most celebrated inventor, Christopher Polhem. In January of 1716, thanks to the efforts of his brother-in-law, Swedenborg went to work with Polhem as his assistant. Polhem was happy with *Daedalus Hyperboreus* and with its young editor—understandably, as Swedenborg had dedicated the inaugural issue to him—and after a short time, he offered Emanuel the hand of his daughter, Maria, in marriage: there is even a story that King Charles XII suggested to Polhem that he do so. Emanuel must have been gratified by the offer. Unfortunately, he preferred Maria's younger sister, Emerentia. Alas, fourteen-year-old "Mrensa," as she was called, favored someone else and rejected Swedenborg. There were other rejections to come: a decade later, in 1726, Swedenborg, who was by this time thirty-seven, asked a pastor for the hand of his daughter but was again rejected.[30] There may have been others that have not been recorded: even so, given Swedenborg's appreciation of women, one wonders why he remained a bachelor. Toksvig suggests that as Swedenborg, being wealthy, had no need of a generous dowry, and in the Sweden of his time, had no need to marry for sex, he probably remained unattached because he did not meet anyone compatible enough for him. Yet Swedenborg himself hints that there may be another reason. The early Swedenborgian C. A. Tulk was an English Member of Parliament, as well as a friend of Samuel Taylor Coleridge. Tulk recounted the story to J. J. G. Wilkinson that Swedenborg had seen his future, heavenly wife in the spirit world. On the earthly plane she was known as the Countess Elizabeth Stierncrona Gyllenborg. Swedenborg had met the Countess when in his early thirties and, presumably, fell in love with her: the closest he could get to her, though, was to become friends with her, her brother and her husband.[31] Swedenborg admitted on more than one occasion that he had had a mistress, and in *Conjugial Love*, written when he was eighty, he argued that "It is useless to list the damage that can be caused and effected by too strict a repression of sexual love in the case of those who are troubled with a superabundance of sexual drive."[32] A "superabundance of sexual drive" seems to have been something Swedenborg devoted much thought to: it is even an issue in heaven. Thankfully, there, angels are in "continual potency," there is no weariness after lovemaking, no postcoital sadness, rather an eagerness of life and cheerfulness of mind. Married angels "pass the night in each other's bosoms," and the wife receives unstintingly "the virile sentiments of the husband." Given Swedenborg's travels, his probable interest in the erotic mysticism associated with Kabbalah, and his own healthy attitude toward sex, we may conjecture that on occasion he relieved himself of some of his potency via the virtues of "pellicacy," an old term for the taking of a mistress. For the rest of the time, he may well have been saving himself for the delights of the conjugial love awaiting him with the Countess in heaven.

Swedenborg worked with Polhem for three years, during which time his mechanical skill was put to great and lasting use. In 1717, Charles XII commissioned Polhem to build a dry dock at Karlskrona, and Polhem brought Swedenborg along to work with him. Swedenborg met the King and the two got along, having many conversations about science and mathematics. At Polhem's request, Charles XII, again impressed by *Daedalus Hyperboreus*, appointed Swedenborg as a special assessor on Sweden's Board of Mines, Swedenborg's one and only professional post. Swedenborg's appointment, however, did not go down well with the other board members, and for the first decade of his new career, he worked without a salary, and had to put up with continual criticism and resentment; along with the example of his father, Swedenborg's experience of his colleagues may have helped shape his interest with hypocrisy. Other important projects that Swedenborg and Polhem tackled were the locks on the Trollhättan Canal, linking Stockholm with the North Sea; Sweden's first saltworks; and a remarkable feat of engineering, in which Swedenborg managed to move the King's navy some fifteen miles across land in order to defeat the Norwegians at Fredrikshald. Although Swedenborg had grown to like Charles XII, his personal feelings did not alter the fact that the King's taste for war was ruining Sweden and creating many enemies within his court. In 1718, Charles XII died from a bullet to the head during the siege of Fredrikshald: to this day there is doubt as to whether the shot came from a Norwegian or a Swedish musket. In any event, with the King's death, Swedenborg's career as an engineer, and his association with Polhem, ended.

Looking at Swedenborg's life, it makes sense that his time as an engineer was short. Although his genius for mechanics is evident, Swedenborg's real passion, his "ruling love" as he would later call it, was for something larger than invention and applied science. He was obsessed with the big, metaphysical questions: the meaning of life, the structure of the cosmos, where infinity ended. And although he applied himself conscientiously to his work as Assessor of Mines, this too seems like something of a duty rather than a pleasure. He had proved himself of "some use" to Sweden, and had shown that his talent for science could produce concrete results. Soon after leaving Polhem, Swedenborg took up his responsibilities as a member of the Swedish Parliament. In 1719 the new queen, Ulrika Eleonora, ennobled the families of Sweden's bishops (this was when the Swedbergs became Swedenborgs) and, as the oldest surviving male of the family, Emanuel took his seat in the House of Nobles. For the rest of his life, Swedenborg would be an active member of the House, and although he never gave speeches, inhibited by his stutter, he contributed important papers on a number of issues: currency reform; trade balances; and mining practices. One of his colleagues in the House, as well as being a fellow assessor, was Count Gyllenborg, the husband of Elizabeth Stierncrona Gyllenborg. In 1720, Swedenborg's stepmother Sara died, and when his share of her estate was settled, he had the assurance of a considerable income for the rest of his life. It would be enough for most people. Swedenborg, however, was not satisfied.

He had always written. There were his early poems, but although his last work before the flood of spiritual and theological writings, *The Worship and Love of God*, was couched in a florid, almost purple prose, he had long abandoned poetry for science. He fulfilled his duties as a statesman and was an exemplary assessor, but Swedenborg's heart and mind lay elsewhere.

Chapter Two: Soul Searching

2

With Charles XII's death in 1718, *Daedalus Hyperboreus* effectively discontinued publication; the last issue would appear the same year. Between then and 1724, Swedenborg, whom one commentator called "the man who had to publish,"[1] produced a few scientific works on a variety of subjects: studies in astronomy, chemistry, what we would today call geology, and miscellaneous writings related to mining. He also produced several memoranda for the Swedish Parliament on the currency, trade, ironworks and other subjects. Swedenborg was an inordinately prolific writer, producing a gargantuan body of material, much of it unpublished in his lifetime. This talent for the written word may have been inherited from his father, who once remarked that ten carts could not contain everything he had written and published.[2]

Swedenborg's enormous output has even led to the suggestion that he was ambidextrous, and when one hand tired of filling blank pages, the other took over. Both hands may have become a bit overtaxed in the mid-1720s, however. In 1724, and continuing for the next decade, Swedenborg seems to have stopped writing, or at least publishing. But in 1734, he returned to the practice that would occupy him for the rest of his long life.

That year, when he was forty-six, Swedenborg published his first major scientific work, a mammoth three-volume opus entitled *Philosophical and Mineralogical Works*. Parts two and three were technical mineralogical treatises dealing in detail with the mining of iron and copper. Part one, however, was different. *The Principles of Natural Things*, or *The Principia*, as it is generally known, was devoted to more metaphysical pursuits. Here Swedenborg presented a general theory about the nature of the universe, how it was formed, and what it is made of. Here he also explored the question of how the finite, physical world can originate in an infinite, immaterial source, i.e., God. This was the beginning of Swedenborg's long quest to find a scientific proof for the reality of the soul.

Ironically, in more recent times, some impressive names in science have attempted to do precisely the same thing, yet their conclusions differ radically from Swedenborg's. For example, when the neuroscientist Nicholas Humphrey goes "soul searching," the title of his 1995 book, his aim is to show that no such thing as the soul exists, and that the "supernatural consolation" offered by belief in the soul is just an illusion we need in order to endure the realities of our existence.[3] And when a more famous figure like Francis Crick, co-discoverer of

DNA, embarked on his own "scientific search for the soul," he returned from his explorations with what he called "the astonishing hypothesis." The hypothesis, Crick tells us, is that our "joys and sorrows, memories, ambitions, sense of personal identity and free will"—everything, that is, that we associate with being meaningful, independent beings—are "nothing more than the behavior of a vast assembly of nerve cells and their associated molecules."[4] Both Humphrey's and Crick's books, and others like them, of which Daniel Dennett's *Consciousness Explained* is probably the most influential, share as a common theme the project of explaining consciousness. They aim to reduce the "mystery of consciousness" to the "problem of consciousness,"[5] a problem that all of the philosophers and scientists who belong to this group believe can be solved through strict scientific—that is, materialist—methods.

Swedenborg was just as scientific as Humphrey, Crick and the rest of the explainers, perhaps even more so, but his premise was different. Although Swedenborg worked at a time when belief in God and the supernatural was being eroded, and although Swedenborg himself weathered some severe storms of doubt, at bottom Swedenborg saw the limitations of the new science being erected out of the work of Newton and Descartes. Where Newtonian science was content to formulate laws out of the evidence offered to the senses, Swedenborg was determined to get behind sensory phenomena in order to arrive at their causes. "The sign that we are willing to be wise," he wrote, "is the desire to know the causes of things, and to investigate the secret and unknown operations of nature. It is for this purpose that each one . . . is eager to acquire a deeper wisdom than merely that which is proffered . . . through the medium of the senses."[6] Like another "spiritual scientist," the Austrian Rudolf Steiner, Swedenborg believed that our inner world, our soul, can be investigated scientifically. For the next decade Swedenborg intended to do just that, his aim being to produce a proof of the soul that the senses themselves would have to accept.

Swedenborg was aided in this quest by a psychological quirk that was linked to the breathing and concentration techniques I spoke of earlier. In his next major scientific work, the title of which is usually translated from the Latin somewhat awkwardly as *The Economy of the Animal Kingdom*, and which deals with the relation between the soul and the body, Swedenborg speaks of an inner experience that one suspects is, in different forms, common among people of genius. Speaking of those he considers the "true men of science," Swedenborg tells us that

> they are exhilarated by the truth, and in the presence of everything that is clear they too are clear and serene. When, after a long course of reasoning, they make a discovery of the truth, straight-away there is a certain cheering light and joyful confirmatory brightness that plays around the sphere of their mind; and a kind of mysterious radiation—I know not whence it proceeds—that darts through some sacred temple in the brain.[7]

This "confirmatory brightness" returned to Swedenborg whenever his meditations brought him closer to the truth. He referred to it as "the sign" and it assumed for him the shape of a flame. It served for Swedenborg a similar purpose to that of the *daimon* that often counseled Socrates. But where Socrates' *daimon* would voice a warning if he should avoid a certain course of action, the presence of Swedenborg's flame was a sign that he was on the right track. Later, in his *Spiritual Diary* and in another work unpublished in his lifetime, *The Word Explained,* Swedenborg recognized that the flame and "cheering light" were indications that he was being guided by spirits; now, however, he took it as a symbol of inner approval. As Wilson Van Dusen, whose work we shall return to later, writes:

> The person who meditates intensely, seeking inner guidance, may find a signal system to guide him. When what he is thinking meets inward approval, the person may suddenly see a flash of light. The light may vary from a pinpoint to a large area, and it is characteristically bright.[8]

Van Dusen points out that Swedenborg's "sign" had nothing to do with the "explosions of light" associated with migraine or, as mentioned earlier, temporal lobe epilepsy. Characteristically these occur as random flashes, starbursts, or a variation of the geometric shapes known as "entopic forms." Swedenborg's flame was a stable, contained image and it appeared only when his thinking was moving in the right direction.

It was important for Swedenborg to understand how our world, which is material and finite and exists in time and space, is linked to its source, which is infinite, non-material, non-temporal and non-spatial. In *The Principia*, Swedenborg answered this riddle by positing dimensionless points as the building blocks, as it were, of the universe. Like those used in geometry, these points have no extension in space. Not being limited to one location, for Swedenborg, they are universally present, existing everywhere. Given this, every portion of our spatial, temporal world can serve as a starting point for a process of inference, which will then lead to the infinite. Within this, all of the apparently separate elements of our world exist in a kind of seamless unity.

In recent times, a similar idea was developed by the physicist David Bohm.[9] Investigating the strange ability of elementary particles to communicate apparently with each other instantaneously, regardless of the distance separating them, and to somehow know each other's position, speed and other factors (which, in a mechanical, Newtonian universe is impossible), Bohm posited what he called the "implicate order." For Bohm this meant that the separateness of our spatial-temporal world, which he calls the "explicate order," is really an illusion, created by our senses. Beneath this explicate order is a deeper underlying reality, the implicate order, which is spaceless, timeless and, like Swedenborg's infinite, unified, possessing what Bohm calls "unbroken wholeness."[10] Given this, Bohm concluded that the elementary particles in his experiments had no need to communicate information about themselves to their counterparts: their separateness, he argued, was illusory. In reality, they were two aspects of the same fundamental unity.

Bohm's vision of an implicate order has often been linked to the work of another scientist, the neurophysiologist Karl Pribram, who developed the idea that the brain works like a hologram. Pribram wanted to know how the brain stores memory, but he soon discovered that none of the standard mechanistic approaches were of any use in understanding this. Although researchers had been trying to locate specific sites for memory storage for decades, they were still drawing a blank. Pribram quickly recognized that the search for specific sites was a mistake; the fact that people with severe head injuries do not automatically lose a definite amount of their memory—say, half, or a quarter—seemed to indicate as much. Increasingly it seemed to Pribram that in storing memory, somehow the *whole* brain was being used, but there was no model for this in the research available. But when he came across an article on holography, Pribram saw the answer. The brain was a kind of hologram.

A hologram is a three-dimensional photograph created by shining a laser beam onto an object, and then bouncing a second laser beam off the light reflected by the first. The pattern of interference created by the two beams is then recorded on photographic film. This pattern appears meaningless until a third laser beam passes through it. When this happens, a three-dimensional image of the original object is produced.

Along with being three-dimensional, a hologram differs from a normal photograph in still another way. If you cut a normal photograph in half, you end up with two halves of one picture. So if you cut a photograph of someone's face in half, the result is two halves of a face. With a hologram, however, when you cut it in half, what you get are two smaller holograms, two smaller faces. And if you cut these halves again, you would get even smaller faces. Like Swedenborg's dimensionless point, the image in a hologram is not localized: it is contained in every part of the whole.

In many ways this arrangement resembles the reiterative structure of the fractals associated with chaos theory. Fractals are the strangely beautiful psychedelic-like patterns formed by charting the course of a mathematical "strange attractor" on an algebraic grid. Discovered by the mathematician Benoit Mandelbrot, they often take on organic, fern-like shapes, which at first seem random but soon reveal a deep order. When the fringes of these mathematical ferns are magnified, it becomes apparent that the smoke-like swirls and curls are really repetitions of the original fractal in miniature. And if the edges of these are themselves magnified, the same is found again. The fractal continues to repeat itself, deeper and deeper into a microscopic infinity.

The holographic and fractal models are very similar to how Swedenborg envisioned the structure of the universe. Swedenborg posited that, as his points were the connecting link to the infinite, they had access to infinite energy, an intuition echoed by later insights regarding particle physics. As we know today, the fundamental elements of the universe are not things, in the sense of hard balls of matter, as the atom was once conceived. The numerous elementary particles making up the physical world are really points of energy, clusters of probability. They are not physical but *mathematical* entities. And the energy packed into these infinitesimal points is, we know, enormous. In Swedenborg's system, the infinite energy of the un-manifest source is constrained in these points,[11] and the points themselves suffer a further constraint by being compelled to move in a definite direction, a vortex or spiral. This step-down approach is in line with the Neoplatonic emanationist system, which Swedenborg came across in his university days. Through a process of stages, an emanation of the Divine gradually transforms itself into the physical world. The movement of Swedenborg's points over time forms a particle, which itself is a further step away from the infinite, and hence subject to more constraint. The particle, too, is compelled to move in a vortex, and its collective movements, at a further step from the infinite, are seen as an atom. The atoms, too, are at a further remove from the infinite, possess less freedom, are compelled to move in a certain way, and in this way eventually form larger and even less infinite bodies. Swedenborg continues to repeat this pattern, eventually arriving at very large bodies like the sun, which he envisions as being made up of many smaller images of itself, much like a hologram or fractal.

*

This reiterative element in Swedenborg's picture of the world has been recognized as an example of "likepartedness." This is a way of seeing the world in which the objects in it, and even the world itself, are made up of smaller versions of themselves. Conversely, the opposite can be true: an object can be part of a larger entity, of which it is a smaller version.[12] We can just as easily say that, for Swedenborg, the sun is made up of innumerable, infinitesimal suns, as we can that for him the sun is really just an immense particle. This idea would repeat itself later on, in Swedenborg's theological writings, when he speaks of the universe as a Grand Man, of which we are all parts. Similarly, Swedenborg's heaven is made up of angels. Once again, this is an idea common to hermetic thought, its basic formula that of the relation between the macrocosm and the microcosm, summed up in the alchemical maxim "as above, so below," which will become something of a running theme in Swedenborg's work.

The similarity between likepartedness, fractals and holograms seems clear, and Swedenborg's ideas also share in the vision of the "Great Chain of Being" that dominated notions of the cosmos in pre-modern thought.[13] But it is also reminiscent of two more recent schemes. In his account of his years with the enigmatic esoteric teacher G. I. Gurdjieff, *In Search of the Miraculous*, P. D. Ouspensky relates the cosmological system at the basis of Gurdjieff's teaching.[14] According to Gurdjieff, who claims to have received the idea from a secret esoteric brotherhood, "The Ray of Creation" proceeds from the Absolute (which seems to me very similar to Swedenborg's Infinite) and, through a series of steps, arrives eventually at the moon, which Gurdjieff posits as the furthest point from the source. The steps in between pass through a kind of cosmic hierarchy: "all worlds," meaning the innumerable galaxies strewn throughout the universe; "all suns," meaning all the stars in our galaxy; "our sun"; "all planets," meaning the other planets in our solar system; and the earth. Each step or, in Gurdjieff's terminology, each octave on the Ray of Creation represents a greater increase in the number of "laws" to which that level is subject. "All worlds," for example, are subject to three laws. We on earth are subject to forty-eight, while the moon is the worst of all, subject to ninety-six. More laws mean less freedom, and this strikes me as very similar to Swedenborg's suggestion that the Infinite proceeds to form our spatial-temporal world through a series of steps that consist of limitations and constraints on itself.

Another system with similarities to this is the *holon* hypothesized by the writer Arthur Koestler.[15] Koestler developed the idea of the *holon* out of his interest in systems theory. We can see it as a pattern of relationship that can be applied to a variety of entities. A *holon* is both a part and a whole: it is a part for that level of the hierarchy above it and a whole for the one below. Its degree of freedom or constraint is determined by the level from which it is perceived. So we can say that while a sentence is a whole of which a single word is a part, the sentence itself is a part of a greater whole, a paragraph, which is itself a part of a still greater one, say a chapter.[16] The single word, which is a part relative to the sentence, is a whole relative to the individual letters, which themselves may be seen as wholes relative to inarticulate gutturals. On a larger scale, London is a whole relative to one of its individual streets, but is itself a part of England, which is again a part of a greater whole, Europe, which is again part of the planet, which is again a part of the solar system, and so on. The spiraling dimensionless points which make up Swedenborg's particles are parts of a whole; those particles, however, are also parts of a greater whole, which is itself a part, and so on.

Swedenborg's hypothesis has a serene beauty and harmony that suggests that, whether or not it is right, it must be fairly close to the truth. He projected the spiraling of his dimensionless points out into the cosmos, and his picture of the Milky Way as a great wheel of stars, spinning around a shared center, anticipated our modern ideas of the galaxy. Other of his intuitions have since been incorporated into our picture of the universe. Although the late-eighteenth-century French mathematician Pierre Simon de Laplace is usually given this honor, there is reason to believe that Swedenborg really should be credited with being the first to posit the nebular hypothesis of solar and planetary formation. It is possible Laplace first encountered the idea through reading Kant, with whom he often shares credit for it, but there is reason to suspect that Kant got the idea from reading Swedenborg, who presents it almost as an afterthought in *The Principia*. After years of neglect, the many intuitions Swedenborg had about the nature of the cosmos, and which have subsequently been taken up by later scientists, were made clear when the Nobel Prize–winning scientist Svante Arrhenius summed up his countryman's contributions to astronomy. Along with the nebular hypothesis of planetary and solar formation, these include the insight that "The earth and the other planets have gradually removed themselves from the sun and received a lengthening time of revolution. . . . The earth's time of rotation, that is to say, the day's length, has been gradually increased. . . . The suns are arranged around the Milky Way. . . . There are still greater systems, in which the milky ways are arranged." To this we can add the notion that stars have axial rotation or spin, and that they circle the Milky Way in a spiral motion. Swedenborg also seems to have anticipated the idea that planets can be formed by the ring of stellar material given off by novae, exploding stars, and he seems to have anticipated also the kinds of stars we now call pulsars, which emit pulses of radiation.[17]

In later years, Swedenborg would have much to say about the possibility of life on other planets. In *The Worlds in Space*, a book written after his crisis, he relates his experiences and encounters with the spirits of the inhabitants of Mars, Jupiter, Saturn and beyond. In the light of this, there is one further contemporary cosmological idea that Swedenborg seems to have anticipated, the "anthropic cosmological principle," developed by John Barrow and Frank Tipler.[18] The anthropic cosmological principle grew out of the recognition of the many cosmic coincidences necessary in order for intelligent life to have appeared on earth: for example, the size of our sun, our distance from it, the presence of our moon, and that of gas giants like Saturn and Jupiter.[19] In its weak form, the anthropic cosmological principle seems to state the obvious: that our universe is one in which intelligent life-forms, such as ourselves, can arise. In its strong form, however, the point is made more emphatically: our universe is one in which intelligent life-forms, like ourselves, *must* arise. Given the structure of our cosmos, the materials it is made of, and the requisite time, some form of intelligent life was bound to turn up, which seems to negate the long-held notion that we are merely chance events. Rather, we seem inevitable. But Swedenborg takes this even further: not only must intelligent life like ourselves arise in our universe, the entire universe was created *in order* for beings like ourselves to exist. And this includes the inhabitants of other planets. This is so because it is through beings like ourselves that heaven is populated. Therefore, the universe was created so that human beings could exist and serve their cosmic purpose by eventually becoming angels and populating heaven. Swedenborg argued that the inhabitants of one planet alone would not suffice for this, and so the cosmos must be filled with other planets harboring intelligent life.

Yet, although Swedenborg had arrived at a rationally acceptable and highly suggestive idea of how the finite is created from the infinite, by the time he had finished *The Principia*, he no longer felt so sure. He was still nagged by the exact nexus or connection between these two incommensurables. In a short work that followed, *The Infinite*, he now declared that the link between the two was Christ. This seems to be an early manifestation of the struggle between the scientific and the religious aspects of his character that would come to a head a decade later. Reason, he now thought, can lead us to recognize that some nexus between the finite and the infinite must exist, but it cannot tell us what it is. This, as they used to say, is the $64,000 question, and even a sympathetic reader like myself comes away from the careful reasoning of *The Principia* still unsure exactly how those dimensionless points arrive in the first place. Mystical accounts like the Kabbalah merely state "that is how things are." But the scientist in Swedenborg wanted to know. Mention of the Christ seems to suggest that Swedenborg was beginning to bump into the limits of science. Toksvig also suggests that at this point Swedenborg had read and been influenced by the work of Jacob Boehme and his followers (although Swedenborg himself denied the claim), for whom nexus was a code word for Christ. In the Christian mythos, Christ certainly filled the role of a meeting point between the earthly and the divine, the finite and the infinite, God made man.

Yet that meeting place was not something one could only reason about: to have true experience of it, it had to be felt. Here Swedenborg begins to approach the existentialism of another, later Scandinavian, Søren Kierkegaard. Toksvig also makes the point that Swedenborg declares that one of the ways in which finite man can experience a taste of the infinite is through "love, or the delight resulting from love." Here Swedenborg is echoing the insight known to poets of all ages, that in passionate human love, we can draw near to an encounter with the Divine. We have already seen that Swedenborg had an interest in erotic spirituality, and we know that in one of his last books, *Conjugial Love*, he made mutually satisfying (and apparently continuous) physical love one of the "delights of wisdom" in heaven. In *Tertium Organum*, P. D. Ouspensky, himself an esoteric philosopher with a scientific bent of mind, remarked that "love is a *cosmic phenomenon*," and spoke poetically about the "contact with the eternal and the infinite which it holds for man." "Love," he tells us, "is the way to sanctity."[20] It seems that Swedenborg, too, had insight into this idea.

But Swedenborg had not given up on science yet. In 1735, Jesper Swedberg died, and Swedenborg was granted another extended leave from his work as an assessor. In 1737, he traveled to Paris to study anatomy and physiology: following this, he did the same in Italy. He also read widely in the anatomical literature of the time: Leeuwenhoek, Malpighi, Willis, Vieussens, and Boerhaave. One product of this time are his writings on the brain, posthumously published as *The Cerebrum*. Another was the aforementioned *Economy of the Animal Kingdom*. Although we can be excused for inferring it from its title, this later work has nothing to do with animals in the wild: the "kingdom" here is the human body, and the "animal" is from the Latin *anima,* meaning the animating energy, or the soul. In these works, Swedenborg made his final all-out assault on locating the elusive "seat of the soul" in the body. This was not an uncommon pursuit: Descartes himself had argued that the soul could be found in the pineal gland, an organ whose function, incidentally, is still not absolutely clear, although it is known to be linked to the production of serotonin, a neurotransmitter. Swedenborg, however, did not agree with Descartes, and he devoted the next seven years of his life to his own investigations. Both *The Cerebrum* and *Economy of the Animal Kingdom* again show how ahead of his time Swedenborg was; among other things, in his work on the brain, Swedenborg made what is probably his most celebrated contribution to neuroscience, the recognition that the gray matter of the cerebral cortex houses higher psychic functions like consciousness, perception, sensation and thought, something that would not be officially recognized until more than a century later.

Swedenborg's tactic was to infer the function of an organ from its structure, and his starting point is one echoed by much of modern neuroscience and philosophy of mind: that the many capacities and abilities of the mind are mirrored in the structure of the brain. For today's scientists, this suggests that the hypothesis of a soul is unnecessary. For Swedenborg, it meant the opposite. Rather than obviate the need for a soul, the incredibly complex arrangement of organic matter housed within our flesh and bones was a clear sign that some intelligence greater than our own was at work. That intelligence Swedenborg called the soul.

But before we look at some of Swedenborg's conclusions, let me give a brief overview of some of his insights into the structure and function of the body and brain that have subsequently been absorbed into the scientific literature. Tedious as this may seem, it compels us to recognize that Swedenborg was not simply a good guesser, and that his work in anatomy and physiology is on a par with other major investigators. We have already mentioned a few of these, but for completeness' sake, the reader, I hope, will not mind some repetition. Michael Stanley has done a great service by collecting them into a concise list. Swedenborg's discoveries, then, include:

1. The coincidence of the motion of the brain with respiration.
2. The independence of animatory motion of the brain and the respiration of the lungs.
3. The extension of the respiratory motion of the brain and lungs to the extremities of the body.
4. The existence of the cerebro-spinal fluid.
5. The circulation of the cerebro-spinal fluid through interstices between the fibers and nerves of the body.
6. The central ganglia and spinal ganglia take over some of the movement initiations of the cerebrum (conditioned reflexes).
7. The existence of the central canal of the spinal cord.
8. The optic lobes are connected with the sense of sight.
9. The seat of consciousness is in the cortical (gray) elements of the brain.
10. The function of the brain is partly as a "chemical laboratory" distributing chemicals through the pituitary gland.
11. The blood is being continually broken down and replaced.
12. The quality of the blood depends upon the organ and the person.
13. The smallest organic particles ("fibers," "cortical elements") are independent centers of forces endowed with individual life.
14. Each organ and "fiber" selects its own requisite nutrients from the blood supplied by the heart's pumping action. (The blood plasma is not *forced* into the tissues, but *drawn* in selectively by the tissues themselves.)[21]

To this we can add that Swedenborg was the first to recognize the existence and importance of neurons and that early on he emphasized the significance of the frontal lobes for the higher psychic functions. A further insight into the brain's structure and function appeared later on in Swedenborg's career, when, having the doors of the spirit world opened to him, and observing that the geography of heaven corresponded to that of the human body, he anticipated the findings of split-brain research, delegating the rational to the left side of the brain and the "affections or things of the will" to the right. Again, the erotic or sexual aspect of Swedenborg's thought can be seen in his recognition that the head and the heart, or the masculine and feminine sides of the mind, need to be integrated. "Peak experiences," as they are called by the psychologist Abraham Maslow, can be seen as a union of these two ordinarily opposing halves: when right and left are brought together, the result is a new, vital and meaningful perception, emphasizing again the sexual character of higher consciousness. Swedenborg also gave importance to a relatively neglected part of the brain, the cerebellum, which is a kind of proto-cerebrum located in the back of the skull. In his later theological writings, it was through the cerebellum that the influx from the Divine enters the soul: this is the reason why in heaven, no one is allowed to stand behind an angel, so as to avoid interfering with the divine flow. Swedenborg's suggestions about the cerebellum, as a kind of contact point between the human and the Divine, were echoed centuries later by the psychologist Stan Gooch, who argued that the cerebellum is the seat of paranormal and mystical experience. Gooch's suggestion that Neanderthal man possessed a larger cerebellum and was hence more mystical than ourselves, parallels Swedenborg's belief that in an earlier time, humankind was closer to the Divine and could perceive its presence directly, unlike ourselves, who are separated from it by our limited rationality. Gooch also makes the interesting remark that, after he had first put forth the suggestion that individuals with marked psychic powers would possess either larger or appreciably more active cerebella, he came across one individual who "reported *actual conscious experience of the cerebellum during . . . paranormal activity*." The individual in question was Swedenborg.[22]

Swedenborg arrived at his conclusion that the body was formed by the soul through his observation of a chick embryo. The prevalent idea at the time was that the embryo consisted of a miniature organism, which simply grew. Swedenborg rejected this, and his rejection is again another of his insights that were subsequently vindicated by later research. But Swedenborg did not accept the modern notion that the development of an embryo into a full-grown organism was a purely mechanical or chemical process. Instead he posited a "formative substance or force" which coordinated the different parts of the embryo into a whole. "The stupendous machine of the animal body," he wrote, "could by no means have come together without a positive directing force." If this were not the case, then, he concludes, we would have to accept that "mighty miracles of formation would result from mere chance." Scientists of the stamp of Jacques Monod, who, in his influential work *Chance and Necessity*, argues precisely that "mighty miracles of formation" *do* "result from mere chance," would scoff at Swedenborg's main insight, that "life is one distinct thing, and nature [which for him meant inorganic matter] is another." Life, for Swedenborg, is concerned with ends and purposes, what in a more technical language is usually called teleology. And nature, or matter, which is subject and slave to the laws of physics, is the means by which life's purposes are carried out.

Anyone conversant with modern biological literature, redolent of selfish genes and random mutations, will know that uttering the "T word"—teleology—is tantamount to declaring oneself a Creationist, or at least a believer in intelligent design. Unfortunately, the "chance or not-chance" debate over the origins and direction of life is too often reduced to a profitless squabble between two rather uninteresting extremes, that of the ultra-neo-Darwinian meaningless process camp, or conversely, that of unintelligent Bible thumping about God's handiwork. Swedenborg's formative substance or force, however, has had some illustrious descendants, and his influence, direct or indirect, can be felt in the speculations and insights of Jean Baptiste Lamarck, Goethe, Alfred Russel Wallace (co-discoverer with Darwin of the theory of evolution through natural selection), Nietzsche, Samuel Butler, Henri Bergson, the vitalist Hans Driesch, George Bernard Shaw, Paul Kammerer, the physicist Erwin Schrödinger, the philosopher Michael Polanyi and Arthur Koestler, to mention a few. Most recently, the work of Rupert Sheldrake and his notion of morphic resonance is a return to Swedenborg's ideas. In *A New Science of Nature* and, more popularly, *The Presence of the Past*, Sheldrake argues that although the discovery of the DNA molecule informs us of the proteins with which an organism is created, it cannot tell us much about how that organism arrives at its distinct form. The same DNA is behind a sunflower, a sequoia and a sixteen-year-old, but the codes that allow each of these to become themselves do not answer the question of why their genetic material develops into their distinctive forms. This is equivalent to recognizing that a Steinway piano, say, is made of wood, ivory, metal and other items, but without offering an explanation as to how these materials are fitted together to form a musical instrument, rather than a heap of stuff. To answer this question, Sheldrake posited the existence of what he calls "morphogenetic fields," immaterial forces that act on the genetic material and shape it. These fields serve a purpose similar to that of the etheric forces of Rudolf Steiner, whose ideas on nature were profoundly influenced by Goethe. Sheldrake's fields are very reminiscent of Swedenborg's formative substance, and in his writings on plant morphology, Goethe made his debt to Swedenborg very clear. Although there are, to be sure, important differences between all the various exponents of non-Darwinian evolutionary ideas, all share the common conviction that mere chance is inadequate as an explanation for both the origin of life and the process of its development. All share in some way Swedenborg's recognition that some essential difference exists between living and dead matter, and that the physical laws which apply to inorganic matter must, in organic matter, accommodate the presence of something else. That something else for Swedenborg was the soul.

*

As we have seen, Swedenborg came across Neoplatonic notions in both his early schooldays and during his exposure to the Cambridge Platonists while in England. The influence of these ideas can be felt in his anatomical work. Swedenborg was faced with the mystery of how an immaterial force can create and inform a material body, and he essayed an answer utilizing the Neoplatonic system of a gradated descent from pure spirit—the Divine—to matter. This descent was a kind of ladder reaching from heaven to earth. Yet, for all his determination to produce a scientific proof of the soul, Swedenborg was forced to recognize the inadequacy of one of science's most cherished beliefs: the continuity of Nature. This belief declares that Nature, that is reality, is of a piece, and the same laws that can accommodate physical reality should also be able to answer any questions regarding anything else. (Another way of putting this is to say that there really is nothing else but physical reality, and anything that seems to be different is just illusory.)

Among other things, the belief in the continuity of nature is behind the drive in contemporary neuroscience to explain consciousness. Seemingly non-material entities like consciousness *must*, it declares, eventually be found to be adequately explained using the same laws as apply to physical phenomena. Living matter is another example. The "vitalist heresy" scoffed at by strict neo-Darwinians argues that living matter is somehow different from non-living matter. Life is something more than another chemical process, however complex it may be; it is different in *kind*, not only degree. One can appreciate why many scientists are reluctant to accept this and to give up the notion that there is no essential difference between living and dead matter: the long-respected principle of Occam's Razor enjoins us not to multiply explanations unnecessarily, and there is an elegance and grace in being able to account for a number of seemingly disparate phenomena with a single theory. Yet one result of this attempt to explain all phenomena using a single set of laws is that in order to accommodate the criteria of science, the phenomena themselves are distorted. Worse still, they are often relegated to being mere illusions, essentially unreal. So, while scientific laws have been more or less very successful at explaining physical phenomena, the phenomena of our inner, subjective worlds have proved less wieldy, and this has led, at different times, to scientists declaring that these phenomena, then, must not really exist. One example is the School of Behaviorism in psychology, which stated that, as it could not be subjected to scientific measurement, there was then no such thing as consciousness, one of the strangest scientific conclusions on record. What is real for science is that which accommodates the criteria of scientific measurement. But how can one measure love, freedom, the good, the true and the beautiful, or any of the other interior experiences that make up what is most meaningful for us? The upshot of this is that for science, that which gives our lives meaning is relegated to the realm of illusion and unreality, and the only real things are some form of physical entity like molecules, atoms and the like. Hence the "astonishing hypotheses" of Francis Crick and others like him.

Many scientists today who recognize this problem shake their heads and say we must face the truth with honesty and rigor. But Swedenborg, and others like him, recognized instinctively that any science that rejects the very things that give life meaning and which motivate us to act, must be mistaken. Accepting such a "truth" would, they knew, be tantamount to suicide, and surely the discipline that promises to free us from superstition, ignorance and false ideas cannot have as its goal the destruction of its practitioners? (The Church saw this danger, I think, and it must have played some part in its opposition to the rise of freethinking, and not only through its desire to retain power and control.) The alternative, Swedenborg recognized, is to alter our ideas about reality.

Swedenborg did just that, and jettisoned the idea of nature's continuity. Nature, he saw, was not all of a piece. There were "breaks" in it, "jumps," the kind of explanatory gaps that many working in consciousness studies today see between the physical structure of the brain and the immaterial phenomena of our interior world. No one has yet shown how we get from a neuron to a thought. The electrochemical charge fired by a brain cell, however intimately and apodictically it may be associated with it, is not the same thing as the image, memory, idea or insight arising in consciousness. We can only weigh thoughts metaphorically, yet a science determined to hold on to its most sacred law would rather ignore this than accept what Swedenborg did: that there was what he called a Doctrine of Series and Degrees which, when applied, could help to make sense of the gaps.

The Doctrine of Series and Degrees recognizes that essential differences exist among different phenomena, which, on the face of it, seems a tautology. Although it is not an example Swedenborg gives himself, we can see what he means if we look at something very close to us: ourselves. In the scientific, materialist view, we are made of atomic and subatomic particles, subject to physical laws, which form into molecules, cells, and so on, until we get to our physical bodies. Although this account gets a little shaky when we reach our thoughts, feelings, etc., it is more or less the accepted version of how we are made. In the esoteric view of human nature, however, things are a bit different. Variations on this scheme can be found, but on the whole the picture goes something like this. Our bodies are made of matter, minerals and the like. But these would lack the requisite form if it were not for what is often called the "etheric body" holding them together. This etheric body serves the function of Swedenborg's formative substance or force. This etheric body, or vital body, is not the same as the material it holds together and animates, and this can be easily seen when observing an organism that has died. Upon death—upon, that is, the absence of the etheric forces—the physical body deteriorates, and breaks down into its component minerals. Yet this etheric body is itself superseded by what is often called the "astral body," which is the seat of our feelings and emotions, our desires, loves and hates. If we had only our physical and etheric bodies, we would be little more than a vegetable. Our astral body gives us our inner life, as it were. Yet this too is not the end, because we have a further element, our ego or "I," the seat of our rational thought, our aims and purposes, which can control our desires and which acts, or should act, as an overall master of our astral bodies. Without this controlling "I" we would be merely a tangle of competing desires, fears and appetites. Another way of seeing this scheme is to recognize it as a part of the chain of being. Here we have minerals, plants, animals and ourselves. Recognizing these other levels in our own makeup, we can appreciate another version of the idea that we are microcosms, little universes.

Now, no amount of matter, however complex, will suddenly become living—although this is how science believes life began in the hypothesized primordial soup—just as no amount of minerals will transform itself into a plant. Likewise, no plant, as far as we know, has desires and appetites in the way that animals have, and no animal, as far as we know, thinks as we do, or possesses an ego in the same way.[23] There is a break between the mineral and the vegetable world, just as there is one between the vegetable and the animal, and the animal and the human. This is not to trumpet our superiority, merely to recognize that in the nature of things, differences not only of degree, but also of *kind,* exist. Swedenborg spoke of these differences as horizontal and vertical, or degrees of breadth and degrees of height. Horizontal differences are differences of degree, the differences, say, between different kinds of matter, or different kinds of animals, or different kinds of plants. Vertical differences are differences in kind, differences between animals and plants, or plants and minerals. Or, as I pointed out earlier, that between a neuron firing an electrochemical charge and the thought associated with it. Another analogy is that between a television set and the program you might be watching on it. You may find the program utter rubbish and decide to throw a brick through the screen. Your television would be broken, but your actions would have no effect on the program. It is not the same thing as the screen. Or, you may find the book you are reading worthless and toss it on the fire. The physical book would surely burn, the pages and binding would crinkle and flare, but the book itself, the novel or story, would be unaffected. The story and the book conveying it—its medium—are, Marshall McLuhan to the contrary, not the same.

Swedenborg would employ his Doctrine of Series or Degrees later, in his theological works, specifically in his use of the notion of correspondences. Here, in *The Economy of the Animal Kingdom*, he uses it to account for how the soul acts on the body; it does so, he declared, not by a continuous medium, but by a series of intermediates, a ladder divided by steps. The exact arrangement of that ladder would lead us into very technical terrain, but we may get an idea of what Swedenborg means through his account of the structure of the psyche.

Swedenborg saw the psyche as made up of four different parts. Earlier he had concluded that there were four kinds of forces (he also called them "auras") in the universe, and he applied a similar scheme in describing the structure of the psyche. The first, or universal, force was the source of gravity; the second force was the source of magnetism; the third force was the ether, which he saw as the source of electricity, light and heat; and the fourth force was the air. These forces originated in the dimensionless points we spoke of earlier, and although inanimate themselves, it was through them that the life force, which flowed from the Infinite, could manifest itself, could, that is, form a body. Following the Doctrine of Series and Degrees, this life force had to descend from the Infinite in the same number of stages or forces. Following this, Swedenborg arrived at a fourfold psyche or soul.

Highest, and corresponding to the first force, was the *anima*, a term that C. G. Jung would later borrow from Swedenborg. This, in a way, was the soul proper. Following Neoplatonic thought, Swedenborg saw the *anima* as distinct from the rational intellect. It was a higher, more intuitive, more spiritual faculty. It is by means of the *anima* that we can obtain a glimpse of the essential unity underlying the world of the senses. The *anima* is the source of order, truth, law, science and beauty, and, perhaps remembering his own experiences of the confirmatory brightness, Swedenborg said that it enters into the level below it, the intellect, in the form of light.

The next level down, the intellectual mind, is formed from the second force or aura. Its business is to understand, to think, to discriminate and to will. If we think of the *anima* as the source of mystical experience, the intellect is that which tries to make sense of the experience, to form it into words. Below the intellect is what Swedenborg called the *animus*, another term borrowed by Jung (although he would interpret both it and the *anima* differently). The *animus* is the seat of our sensuous desires, rather like the astral body mentioned above, and it is formed from the material of the third force. Last is the realm of our senses themselves, which are anchored in the material of the fourth and final force.

Although Swedenborg devised this fourfold scheme—which is similar in many ways to the esoteric view of human nature mentioned above—in essence the real distinction is between the soul and the body, or what he also called the internal and external man. These two poles or extremes are involved in a constant struggle. The *animus* prompts us to give in to our appetites, our habits, our sensual desires and comforts; it wants, more or less, to lead an easy animal existence. It is lazy and seeks immediate gratification. Although by itself it can offer little resistance to the temptations of animal existence, the intellect, or *mens*, is, however, open to the influx from the *anima*. It can heed the call of our higher self, as it were, listen to its exhortations to the spiritual life and, in doing so, strive to control and order the lower passions. We can look at the *anima* as the source of our highest values, the ethical, moral and spiritual perceptions that motivate us to act out of something more than our own selfish appetites and needs. The *mens* is neutral: it can show us how to go about something, can understand the logic involved, but by itself it can provide no meaning or motivation. (So, while it can tell us the best way to get from A to B, it cannot tell us why we should go there.) Our senses are the means by which we perceive the physical world and, like the *mens*, are neutral: they simply provide information. It is with the *animus*, however, that we must struggle.[24]

Yet we must not think of Swedenborg as condemning sensual desire. We have seen how important sexual love was for him. Desires were not to be expunged, but moderated. Those who tried to repress or kill the passions were, he believed, as bad as those who gave in to them absolutely. The soul had not created the body in order to torment it, Swedenborg realized, and later, when he described the geography of the higher worlds, he saw that those spirits who chose to be celibate lived on the periphery, not the center of heaven. Swedenborg himself was a sensually aware man living in a sensual age, and it would have seemed unhealthy, to say the least, for human beings to torture themselves over promptings that were only natural. Swedenborg was also a very practical man, with an eye for the *use* of something, and desire and the less carnal appetites had their uses too. A mind enlightened as to the proper means of gratifying the lower appetites could, with discipline and discrimination, harmonize the yearnings of the *animus* so that it no longer sounded a raucous call for immediate satisfaction, but instead lent its voice to a well-rounded experience of life. In this Swedenborg was not very different from other worldly men of his time.

Although the references to sex in his *Journal of Dreams* have often attracted a disproportionate amount of interpretation, it was not with the body and its needs that Swedenborg felt most obliged to struggle. His ambition, his ego, his self-love: it was with these manifestations of the external man that his own internal man was about to lock horns. These two sides of Swedenborg's soul were about to collide in what seemed, at times, a life-and-death struggle. And as so often happens in battles of this sort, the outcome would do nothing less than change his life.

Chapter Three: The Night Sea Journey

3

Our most important document concerning the period of Swedenborg's crisis is his remarkable *Journal of Dreams*. Swedenborg made it a practice to keep a diary during his many travels, and the opening pages of his journal for the years 1743–4 begin in much the same way as his other travel diaries. Swedenborg was a keen traveler, and his appetite for new sights, new experiences and new acquaintances was great. But his travel diaries, while they provide much important information about his journeys, have, unlike those of his near contemporary William Beckford,[1] little literary value, being more or less a record of where he went, what he saw and whom he met. Yet toward the end of 1743, his diary takes on a new and different character. As early as 1734, Swedenborg had shown a deep interest in dreams, sparked by his reading of a work on psychology by the philosopher Christian Wolff. Stimulated by Wolff's ideas, Swedenborg began to pay close attention to his own dreams. In doing so, he reached some fascinating conclusions. For one thing, he saw that, contrary to what Wolff had asserted, he was able in his dreams to remember things that had escaped him while awake. For example, Greek and Hebrew words that he had consciously forgotten would return to him while asleep. He also noted that, although Wolff was correct to suggest that dreams are associated with bodily sensations, they are not simply the effects of some physical cause. Dreams, Swedenborg saw, often "tend to some definite end." They are not random, meaningless fantasies, sparked by some physical process, but are products of the soul. Dreams, Swedenborg realized, "were directed by one of whose origin we are ignorant—a circumstance which often seems to us a matter of wonder."[2]

If this seems a remarkable anticipation of Freud's ideas, it is even more so an early insight into Jung's notions about the Self, the central psychic archetype and the creative hand behind our dreams. For Freud, dreams are symbols portraying desires and wishes that, were we to recognize them truthfully, would shock us. They have, for him, a negative character, being a kind of camouflage, hiding our secret thoughts from ourselves; hence the need for the psychoanalyst to uncover their true meaning. For Jung, however, dreams are not a substitute for something else, but a symbolic message from the Self; their job is to guide our conscious egos toward a more unified awareness, and they often present our conscious selves with insights into our potentials of which we are usually ignorant. For Jung too, just as for Swedenborg, dreams "tend to some definite end," that end being what Jung called "individuation," the gradual and lifelong maturation of the ego so that it transcends itself and integrates with the wider Self. As the psychotherapist Stephen Larsen has recognized, Jung's "individuation" has much in common with Swedenborg's teaching of "regeneration," which is essentially a kind of spiritual rebirth.[3] Dreams, then, are one means by which the soul leads us to the experiences and encounters necessary for our spiritual salvation, a truth of which Swedenborg was to have a more than abstract awareness.

Exactly when in 1743 Swedenborg began to record his dreams is unclear. He notes that on August 20 of that year, he traveled from Bremen to Leer through Oldenburg, which, he tells us, "is a country belonging to the King of Denmark." He passes by a fort, then through a large town, Groningen, and in Leeuwarden he sees the Princess's palace.[4] Nothing exceptional in this, it is all very informative and not unlike many a Fodor's guide. Then, after reaching Harlingen, which is "a large town," there is a gap. Several blank pages remain, and there is evidence that a few others have been torn out. Then we have several undated entries, dealing entirely with his dreams, as well as his trance states, and the curious cessation of both his interest in sex and his ambitions about his scientific work, until March 1744, when Swedenborg's dream journey is in full swing.

Swedenborg's *Journal of Dreams* was not the first of his diaries upon which a person or persons unknown—possibly Swedenborg himself—did some hasty editorial work regarding his dreams. In another dream diary for 1736–9, other pages had been likewise unceremoniously extracted. The reason for this was almost certainly the same as caused the uproar surrounding the publication of the 1743–4 dream diary in the mid–nineteenth century: the unambiguously sexual character of several entries. In our time of kiss-and-tell tabloids and raunchy "lad" magazines, when it is possible to view real people having real sex on reality TV, the frank inclusion in a private journal of the kinds of dreams practically all of us have does not bat an eye, and the minimal description Swedenborg devotes to them is barely worthy of comment. But in less unbuttoned times this was not the case, and in the first English edition of the journal, the few dreams of an erotic type were published in Latin. More than likely, the reason for trying to obscure these sexual dreams of Swedenborg's is the less than saintly personality they suggest, pointing to the fact that, along with being an important theological thinker, Swedenborg was also a man. Anyone who pays attention to his or her own dreams will be familiar with the raw, often very crude (and rude) character they take; this suggests that we either have a real but hidden appetite for some of the things depicted, or that our unconscious (or Self or soul) does not want to waste time and gets right down to business, employing the most direct imagery possible. In any case, as has been pointed out, Swedenborg was interested in sex, and given this it would be unusual, and actually more cause for comment, were it to be absent from his dreams.

Perhaps we should briefly address these sexual dreams at the start, leaving us free to move on to other things. Probably the most commented on are two dreams in which Swedenborg encounters a motif made common by psychoanalytical literature, the *vagina dentata*, a vagina with teeth. In April 1744, Swedenborg dreamed that he "lay with one that was by no means pretty, but still I liked her. She was made like others; I touched her there, but found at the entrance it was set with teeth."[5] In another dream of October the image recurs: "Saw in vision a coal fire brightly burning, *which signifies the fire of love*. Afterward I was in company with women who had teeth on a certain place which I wished to penetrate, but the teeth interfered."[6] Clearly, this is imagery a Freudian would recognize, and Jungians too have ventured the idea that Swedenborg's intense rationalism led him to undervalue his natural desires, hence the threatening character of the dreams. Yet Swedenborg's own interpretations differed. In the first instance, something about the woman reminded him of a politician he knew, and from this Swedenborg thought that the dream meant that he should either have no business with women (which by this time seems to have been the case anyway, as he states at the beginning of the journal that his interest in women has faded), or that he should avoid politics. In the other dream, Swedenborg believed the *vagina dentata* indicated that he was busy with some sort of work that he should not regard as a "plaything."[7] Throughout most of the diary, Swedenborg interprets his dreams in light of his scientific work, and it is only gradually and, it has to be said, painfully that he begins to understand that something else is involved.

There were other, less threatening sexual dreams too. Again in April 1744, a few weeks after a dream of a different sort, which we will return to shortly, Swedenborg dreamed that something "holy" was dictated to him, which ended in *"sacrarium et sanctuarium."* Then,

> I found myself lying in bed with a woman, and said, "Had you not used the word *sanctuarium*, we would have done it." I turned away from her. She with her hand touched my member, and it grew large, larger than it had ever been. I turned around and applied myself; it bent, yet it went in. She said it was long. I thought during the act that a child must come of it.[8]

Yet other dreams, the majority, lack any erotic element, and are much more harrowing. In one he is trapped by the spokes on a machine, and is swung off the ground, unable to escape. In another he is in a beautiful garden, and he wishes to buy a section of it for himself. But then he sees someone picking invisible insects and killing them. The person explains that they are infesting the people in the garden; Swedenborg then sees that one of the insects falls from himself onto a white linen cloth. It was, he believed, his own "uncleanness." In another dream he descends a great staircase at the bottom of which is an abyss; people on the other side want to help him across, but he cannot quite reach them, and he awakens, believing the dream "signifies the danger I am in of falling into hell."[9] Other dreams suggest a similar predicament. In one he is atop a mountain, with a great gulf yawning below. He tries to pull himself up to avoid falling, but cannot. In another, a woman lies down beside him. She tells him that she is pure, but that he "smelled ill."[10] When he asks in a dream for a cure for his sickness, he is given a bundle of rags. In another dream he struggles with a serpent, which turns out to be the dog of an acquaintance who is fond of the good life ("luxury, riches, vanity") and who is trying to seduce him to enjoy the same. Swedenborg tries to hit the snake-dog with a club, but misses, and in the end he strangles it and squeezes its nose until poison squirts out.[11]

*

The psychologist Wilson Van Dusen has written extensively on Swedenborg's dream journal, and his conclusion is that, through his own interest in observing them, Swedenborg's dreams brought about a change in his personality. "The central change that takes place in the *Journal of Dreams*," Van Dusen writes, "is that the very basis of [Swedenborg's] understanding was shifted by this inward exploration."[12] That change, Van Dusen suggests, was from an intensely rational, detached and "objective" sensibility—what we usually associate with a scientist or philosopher—to one that was "affectional" and "living." Swedenborg's sexual dreams were not the product of repression or some sort of fear of the female, as the *vagina dentata* might suggest. Taking his cue from Jung, Van Dusen believes that the erotic and feminine character of some of Swedenborg's dreams was aimed at awakening his feeling side, which had long been obscured (repressed perhaps) by his devotion to science.

Yet it was Swedenborg's own passionate interest in science that cleared the way for his entrance into the inner worlds. Swedenborg's "journey into the interior," in the literary critic Erich Heller's apt phrase, was greatly enhanced by his remarkable powers of concentration, and his peculiar habit of controlling his breath. His ability to focus on a problem and to block off the distractions of the external world allowed Swedenborg to open the doors of perception, and to enter the world of dreams, visions and ecstatic states with an ease most of us would find impossible. Again, we have to remember that Swedenborg had been practicing breath control since he was a young boy, and that by the time of his *Journal of Dreams*, he had been familiar with unusual states of consciousness for half a century. There was the confirmatory brightness we have mentioned, as well as the visions of his childhood playmates. Swedenborg was not as unfamiliar with inner states as his devotion to science might suggest, and we know that his great aim at this point was to prove the existence of the soul scientifically. But what Van Dusen is saying is that, as Swedenborg became more and more involved in his inner world, the idea that he could observe its processes as an outsider became less and less tenable. It was, after all, his own inner world he was venturing into, which is another way of saying that he was venturing into himself. And however detached, dispassionate and objective we may be while observing ourselves, in the end we are not solely sober recording instruments. We are living beings, a fact the implications of which Swedenborg was perhaps just beginning to grasp.

He had already had a taste of it, as evidenced by his insight in *The Infinite* that the experience, and not simply the recognition, of Christ as the nexus between the finite and the infinite was crucial. But Swedenborg's was no sudden conversion, and he returned to the work he had been engaged in for decades. He had written an enormous amount on the brain, and had planned a continuation of *The Economy of the*

Animal Kingdom that would be even longer than the initial work. These were his concerns at the beginning of his dream journal, and it was in light of these works that he interpreted his early experiences in the interior. Although he tells us that his "interest, and self-love in my work had passed away,"[13] Swedenborg still felt that he could accomplish something great and that his scientific work would be successful. Yet it must have been clear to him that he would never find the soul in the manner he had hoped he would, at the point of a scalpel or the end of a syllogism. It was a mistake even to think he would find it at all. Rather, it seemed that it had come looking for him.

As Van Dusen argues, the process of "going within," of inner exploration, of attentiveness to dreams and other psychic processes, brings about a change in the center of gravity of the personality. One need not be a scientist or as decidedly intellectual as Swedenborg for this to be a profitable pursuit. Along with many other thinkers, Van Dusen recognizes that for some time now, Western culture has valued the rational aspects of the mind over the intuitive and emotional, with the result that these neglected areas have suffered, leaving us with a sense of alienation from the world and of being, as the novelist Walker Percy put it, "lost in the cosmos." In popular terms, we are all more "left" brain than "right," and the imbalance needs to be corrected.[14] This is not a new development. Starting just after Swedenborg, we can chart an ongoing resistance to the "scientification" of human experience that includes people like William Blake, Goethe, the Romantics, on up to such disparate twentieth-century examples as existentialism and New

Age philosophy.[15] Space does not allow me to pursue this important question here; suffice it to say that, as I discussed earlier regarding the attempt of many neuroscientists and philosophers of mind to explain consciousness, the central gesture of science, its method of arriving at truth, is to eject all that it considers subjective from the phenomenon under scrutiny. What remains, leached of all subjectivity, it considers true, which really is another way of saying that what remains is susceptible to scientific measurement. Yet what science leaches out of its objects of study is the very thing that gives meaning to our experience. Put briefly, the whole project of "going within," which arguably we can trace back to humankind's first awareness of itself, is an attempt to reintroduce subjectivity, and hence meaning, to our experience of the world.[16]

Swedenborg, however, did not see it in these abstract terms. We have to remember that, although seeing it in this way may help us to put the phenomenon in perspective, the actual experience, the process of "going within," is something different. We may gain some benefit in understanding our emotional life by absorbing books on personal relationships, but the heartaches and agonies of love are raw and immediate, not abstract. Swedenborg did not see "going within" as a means of becoming acquainted with his right brain. For him it was the way toward God. Most of us may not be prepared to follow him in this. For us, it may be enough to recognize the need to journey deeper within, to become acquainted with aspects and parts of ourselves of which we are usually unaware. That is fine: Swedenborg did not live in a time when ideas about transpersonal psychology and self-actualization were fairly common. He lived in a time when religion was still the central experience of people's lives. The deeper Swedenborg entered the interior worlds, the clearer became the lesson he was being taught: he had to give up the belief in his own powers, to relinquish any thought that he might be able to accomplish anything on his own, and make himself open to the Lord.

This, as we might suspect, was not easy. Swedenborg speaks of temptation. The temptation here is not the kind we might imagine. It was not the temptation of worldly goods and riches; Swedenborg was in any case well off and could afford most luxuries. The temptation was his self-love, his belief that through his own efforts, he could accomplish something, could save himself. His dreams told him otherwise. He was being put through the mill, faced with his own high self-regard, and being shown that it was worthless. This is an aspect of Swedenborg's thought that has put many readers off, even those, like Emerson, who hold him in high esteem. For Swedenborg, we can *do nothing on our own*. Any good we do, any worthwhile acts we may accomplish, are done through us by the Lord. We are, as Swedenborg declared, vessels. What Swedenborg went through during his crisis was more or less the emptying of himself, so that his vessel would be open to the influx of the Lord. Personally, while I can appreciate the need to jettison our self-love, in the sense of a childish absorption in our own needs and desires to the detriment of others, I am less able to follow Swedenborg in his insistence on our inability to do any good on our own. I am not sure if it makes any real difference whether, when some good is accomplished through me, I, or some other agent, is responsible. But an emphasis on our weakness and inherent evil may lead to an attitude of apathy and despair. Clearly this is not Swedenborg's message; his doctrine of use and his ethical entreaty to "Do the good that you know" forcefully argue otherwise. Swedenborg's ethic is one of activity and the fruitful employment of one's powers, yet his insistence that, without the Lord, we are essentially evil remains open to abuse.

*

This, however, was Swedenborg's struggle. He was afflicted with "double thoughts," a very concrete expression of his being in two minds. No sooner did he come to some conclusion about his predicament than its opposite came to him and proved to be equally final and decisive. He oscillated between belief and doubt, moving from the confirmatory brightness of his inner light, into the dark night of the soul. Other phenomena disturbed him too, such as the precognitive or prophetic dreams he seemed to have. A deep melancholy set in, and Swedenborg even began to wonder about his sanity. Outwardly, he remained as always, and in the summer of 1743, he had again petitioned the Board of Mines for a leave of absence, so that he could travel to Amsterdam and oversee the publication of the first two parts of his new work, *The Animal Kingdom*. But inwardly Swedenborg was clinging on for life.

In his masterpiece *The Varieties of Religious Experience*, the philosopher William James, whose father, Henry James, Sr., was a follower of Swedenborg, wrote about the travails of the "sick soul." For these "twice born" individuals, James tells us,

> evil is no mere relation of the subject to particular outer things, but something more radical and general, a wrongness or vice in his essential nature, which no alteration of the environment, or any superficial rearrangement of the inner self, can cure, and which requires a supernatural remedy.[17]

Swedenborg himself could have written this. It was certainly something he felt. In his diary he noted down an incident which tells us much about his state of mind at this time. Sitting at a table in an eating house, Swedenborg heard a man

> ask his neighbor the question whether anyone could be melancholy who had more than enough money. I smiled inwardly and would have answered, if it had been proper to do so in that company or if I had been asked, that a man who has more than enough of everything may not only be subject to melancholy but to a still deeper kind which is that of the mind and the soul or of the spirit which effects it; I wondered that he brought it up. I can bear witness to this so much the more since I by the grace of God have been granted an abundance of all that I need temporally; I could live well on my income alone and carry out what I have in mind and still have money left over; therefore I

can bear witness that the sadness or melancholy which comes from a lack of means is of a lower and a physical kind and in no way equal to the other.[18]

Dry and not a little abstract, but it conveys a sense of a man facing a despair that no material palliative could ease, although today he would more than likely be prescribed any number of antidepressants.

Swedenborg's crisis came to a head in the night of April 6–7, 1744. He had been reading about the miracles God performed through Moses, but his doubts about the truth of the Bible seemed relentless, and he understood why "the angels and God showed themselves to shepherds, but never to the philosopher that lets his understanding take part in the matter." The understanding, the intellect, asks niggling questions like why God "used the wind when he called the locusts together? Why he hardened Pharaoh's heart? Why he did not do all at once?"[19] These same types of question are asked today by people of a debunking sensibility, who harp on about the logical inconsistencies in biblical accounts of, say, the Creation, wondering how we can speak of the first day before God had even made the sun, or whether Adam and Eve had navels. Swedenborg himself had an acute critical intelligence, and he would never suggest that we accept the literal sense of the Bible as true—indeed, Swedenborg believed that his mission was precisely to show the error of this. Yet he also recognized that such "clever" inquiries miss the point, and understood why shepherds and children are more apt to see angels than are so-called "wise men." The intellect of the wise men gets in the way, and tries to use logic to grasp an experience that exceeds it. Rejecting the literal truth of revelation, they themselves remain all too literal; they may score points by showing up flaws in this or that Bible story, but this very practice reveals a kind of spiritual autism. "The mind is the slayer of the real," the Upanishads tell us, and Swedenborg knew this, as all mystical and spiritual thinkers do, intuitively. It was precisely to get past his own formidable intellect that he was going through this crisis.

Let us try to imagine Swedenborg's state. For weeks he had been passing through ecstasies in which he "heard speech that no human tongue can utter,"[20] and agonies of "wretchedness as of final condemnation, as of being in hell."[21] He also suffered spells of swooning, fainting fits and uncontrollable trembling. On the night of April 7, after struggling with his "double thoughts" for hours, Swedenborg went to bed. Soon he heard a noise under his head—by this time it was a familiar experience. He thought this was "the tempter" leaving him for the night. Then suddenly, he felt a violent shuddering, and a sound like thunder. He fell asleep, but was awoken a few hours later by another fit of shaking, and more thunder, this time accompanied by a great rush of wind.[22] The attack was so powerful it threw him out of bed and onto the floor, facedown, and he seems to have then had something like an out-of-body experience.[23] There he found himself asking Christ to make him worthy of his grace: the words, he tells us, "were put into my mouth." Then he felt a hand grasp his, and he found himself in Christ's bosom, "face to face." It was "a face of holy mien, and in all it was indescribable, and he smiled so that I believe that his face had indeed been like this when he lived on earth." Christ then asked Swedenborg if he had a "clean bill of health": an allusion to Swedenborg's close shave with a hangman's noose on his first trip to London. Swedenborg answered that he, Christ, knew the answer to this better than he did, to which Christ answered, "Well, do so," which Swedenborg understood to mean "Do what thou has promised."[24] This is the first instance in which Swedenborg seems to have received an injunction from the Lord to perform some task.

According to Van Dusen, the "promise" Swedenborg had made was to abandon his scientific work and to continue on his voyage within. He did, but not immediately; all during these experiences, Swedenborg continued to go about his work, seeing his new writings ready for publication. Van Dusen remarks that it was important that Swedenborg "had a set of values and struggled against inner tendencies that he did not consider acceptable."[25] He did not merely "give way," abandoning himself to strange forces. For one thing, Swedenborg was on guard against "the tempter" and the evil spirits who, he knew, could disguise themselves as angels. Almost two centuries later, C. G. Jung would embark on his own "night sea journey" into the uncharted depths of his unconscious, following his break with Freud. Jung, too, went through some harrowing experiences,[26] and there is little doubt that like Swedenborg, had Jung not had a solid, stable ground to support him—in his case, his family and medical practice—he may have been overwhelmed by what was, from all accounts, something close to a psychotic episode. Both men passed through what the historian of psychology Henri Ellenberger called a "creative illness," from which they emerged with new insights and a deeper understanding of human experience.[27]

Dreams, even those as powerful as Swedenborg's, are not necessarily a sign of mental imbalance. Yet when dream states start to cross the line into waking life, we begin to wonder. Van Dusen suggests that many of Swedenborg's visions came to him in the hypnagogic state, a period between sleep and waking in which consciousness seems to hover in a kind of half-dream. Many writers, poets, musicians, philosophers, psychologists and others have explored this curious state of consciousness.[28] The difference between dreams and hypnagogic states is that in hypnagogia the conscious ego remains alert and can communicate and interact with the vision; unlike in dreams, one can observe inner processes without becoming absorbed in them. The visions seem to take place "out there"; in hypnagogia, one remains aware of the external world, yet can also observe inner experience. Given the extraordinary length of the *Spiritual Diary*, Van Dusen is probably right when he says that "Swedenborg explored the hypnagogic state more than anyone else has before or since."[29] Swedenborg apparently had the ability to remain in this state for hours, and it is not surprising that this began to have an effect on his waking states. In the *Spiritual Diary*, Swedenborg has an entry in which he relates an experience that suggests that the membrane separating the waking world from the inner landscapes he was exploring was becoming permeable. He writes that during a stay in London:

> At mid-day, about dinner time, an angel who was with me spoke to me saying that I was not to indulge the belly too much at table. While he was with me there then clearly appeared to me, as it were, a vapor exuding from the pores of my body like something watery, in the highest degree visible, which slipped down to the ground where a carpet was seen upon which the collected vapor was turned into various little worms, which being gathered together under the table, were burned up in a moment, with a loud noise or sound: the fiery light therein was seen by me and the sound heard.[30]

This incident held much meaning for Swedenborg, and a somewhat different version of it appeared many years later, in an account by Swedenborg given to Carl Robsahm, a friend of his late years. In this version, the angel has become a man who appears out of nowhere, and the worms are joined by "horrid crawling reptiles, . . . snakes, frogs, and similar creatures." Swedenborg says he was perfectly conscious, and his thoughts clear, but when he saw that he was no longer alone, he felt frightened by the mysterious stranger, who proceeded to advise him to "Eat not so much."[31] At which point, everything went black, and when his vision cleared, the man had disappeared. Swedenborg was so struck by the encounter that he hastened to his lodgings. He was convinced that what had happened was not a chance event, and as if to make this point certain, the man appeared again, this time in his room. He told Swedenborg that he was the Lord God, the Creator of the World and the

Redeemer, and that he had chosen Swedenborg for a crucial task: to reveal the spiritual sense of the Scripture, which he himself would make clear to him. This, more than anything else, was the turning point of Swedenborg's later life. He told Carl Robsahm,

> That same night were opened to me so that I became thoroughly convinced of their reality, the worlds of spirits, heaven, and hell, and I recognized there many acquaintances of every condition in life. From that day I gave up the study of all worldly science, and labored spiritual things, according as the Lord commanded me to write. Afterward the Lord opened, daily very often, my bodily eyes, so that, in the middle of the day I could see into the other world, and in a state of perfect wakefulness converse with angels and spirits.[32]

Swedenborg was so moved by this event that he even abandoned the book he was working on at the time. *The Worship and Love of God* was far from scientific; it was the closest thing to poetry that Swedenborg had written for decades, a sudden eruption of the spiritual and religious emotions he had been struggling with. Written in a lush, purple poetic prose, it was Swedenborg's retelling of the Creation and of the events in Paradise, and although suffused with Neoplatonic philosophy, it was couched in the kind of erotic spirituality that had attracted him on more than one occasion. As Adam and Eve are about to embark on the conjugial union which awaits us all in heaven,

They met nothing which did not fill all the senses with the pleasantness of beauty, and at the same time everything gave opportunity for conversation and turned this first experience of their lives into intimacy; from which the youth could not but turn the conversation to the testification of his love. For all things were in vernal flower and genial sport, and as it were enticed the pledges of union with the love which burned to hasten the unition of the associate mind. Everything was auspicious, heaven itself favoring; wherefore no delay interposed until the bride also burned with a like torch of mutual love and declared herself as favorable and pleased at the coming of her bridegroom.[33]

Not a bodice ripper certainly, but more affectional than anything coming from Swedenborg's pen for some time. This passage also makes clear that Swedenborg's ideas about love anticipated the Romantic infatuation with Woman as the "eternal feminine" that would overrun Europe in the early nineteenth century. The idea of the "soulmate," initiated in Plato's *Symposium*, and carried on by the troubadours and the chivalric tradition, reached a height with the Romantics, superseded only by the schmaltzy love stories emerging out of Hollywood. And it may not be going too far to suggest that the promise of conjugial love found in Swedenborg's writings is echoed in the booming Internet dating business of the early twenty-first century, with its guarantee of "finding that special someone." But even this outpouring of sensuous bliss and tremulous feeling could not accommodate the change in

Swedenborg. Something totally new was needed, and that's exactly what came about.

*

During his lifetime, Swedenborg was accused of being mad by his detractors, and an attempt was made to have him declared insane and put in an asylum. This failed, as did an attempt to charge him with heresy, yet once it was evident that Swedenborg, who had published his theological works anonymously, was the man who had written about his journeys to heaven and hell, the question of whether he was crazy or not became a popular topic. After Swedenborg's death, a Swedish clergyman named Mathesius, who was hostile to Swedenborg's teachings, collected some gossip from one of Swedenborg's London Moravian landlords. According to him, on at least one occasion Swedenborg had run into the street in his nightshirt, waving his hands in a fit of delirium, talking strangely about angels; he also seemed to have had a period of compulsive behavior, spending an inordinate amount of time washing his feet.[34] Given that this anecdote was recorded by an enemy, we can, I think, take it with a few grains of salt. Yet a reader of the *Journal of Dreams* and the *Spiritual Diary* cannot be blamed for wondering exactly what was happening to Swedenborg.

Evil spirits attempt to possess parts of his body: they speak to him; he speaks to himself for long periods; he describes seeing angels and spirits hovering before him, pinpointing their location with exactness; he speaks with the dead; foul odors envelop him; he travels to other planets; he speaks with the Apostles.[35] His physical condition bears considering too: he sleeps for twelve hours at a stretch, and sometimes stays in bed for three or four days at a time; he is subject to swoons; he experiences "night sweats" and fits of trembling; his "double thoughts" exhaust him. And his moods swing from feeling he is the greatest of sinners to basking in heavenly grace. Add to this the central claim that he, Swedenborg, had been singled out by Christ to reveal to humankind the true meaning of Scripture, and it is not difficult to find words like "delusional," "megalomaniacal" and "Messiah complex" coming to mind. Clearly this is the sort of thing that most of us would consider evidence of mental imbalance, and over the years others have felt similarly; not only strict rationalists, which would not surprise us, but fairly open-minded individuals, like the existential philosopher Karl Jaspers, and the "spiritual scientist" Rudolf Steiner.[36] Yet to those who knew him, Swedenborg showed no signs of madness, even though for years "in company with other men, I spoke just as any other man, so that no one was able to distinguish me either from myself as I had been formerly, or from any other man; and, nevertheless, in the midst of company I sometimes spoke with spirits." We need to remember that the company Swedenborg kept at this time included other members of the Swedish Board of Mines, other statesmen in the Parliament, publishers, printers, and many other men of high professional and social standing. So normal did Swedenborg appear to his colleagues that in 1747 he was recommended unanimously by the Board of Mines to fill the seat of Councilor of Mines recently made vacant, a position just short of President of the Board. Swedenborg, however, desiring to devote all his time to his "mission," graciously requested that the King should not appoint him, and that he should be pensioned on half his salary instead. The entire Board expressed its regret at having lost so conscientious an assessor. A full four years into his journey within, had Swedenborg been a raving lunatic, one imagines he would have been laid off, not headhunted for a top-flight position.

As I said, Swedenborg himself questioned his mental state at times. But having given the idea due thought, he decided that although on occasion he might have been a candidate for it, he remained in possession of his faculties, and he even came up with a few definitions of madness, which he applied to himself. One recipe for madness, he remarked, was to spend too much time alone, pondering on the deep questions of existence. Such preoccupation led to his "double thoughts" and to the kind of mental and spiritual paralysis that T. S. Eliot wrote of in his poem "Ash Wednesday":

> And pray that I may forget
> These matters that with myself I too much discuss
> Too much explain[37]

Unlike Eliot, Swedenborg did not want to "forget," but to push beyond the paralysis, to continue the journey within. Although it would be easy to list the many mundane and demanding activities that Swedenborg continued to engage in, and to gather testimony from his contemporaries as to his eminently rational deportment, to my mind the clearest evidence of Swedenborg's sanity is the phenomenology of inner states he developed during his inner voyages. Again, if Swedenborg was simply rattling on about seeing angels and evil spirits, we would expect a more or less monotonous account. What we get, however, is a meticulous cartography of inner states, something similar to the conscientious diaries he kept of his outer journeys. Earlier I mentioned hypnagogia; here is Swedenborg's description of this unusual state of consciousness:

> But different is the vision which comes when one is in full wakefulness, with the eyes closed. This is such that things are seen as though in clear day. Nay, there is still another kind of vision which comes in a state midway between sleep and wakefulness. The man then supposes that he is fully awake, as it were, inasmuch as all his senses are active. Another vision is that between the time of sleep and the time of wakefulness, when the man is waking up, and has not yet shaken off sleep from his eyes. This is the sweetest of all, for heaven then operates into his rational mind in the utmost tranquility.

Swedenborg called being in this state "passive potency," indicating a kind of relaxed alertness, a condition of observant receptivity. It was not the only state he was familiar with. In an entry in his *Spiritual Diary*, Swedenborg maps out four distinct types of "sight," as he calls these different "altered states of consciousness."[38] These do not exhaust the different interior terrains he explored, but his account gives us an idea of how carefully he observed what was happening to him during his journey within. The first sight is "the sight during sleep, as vivid as that of daytime, so that in sleep itself I would say that if this were sleep, wakefulness would also be sleep." This last remark reminds us of the belief of another esoteric teacher, G. I. Gurdjieff, that what we take to be our "waking state" is really only another form of sleep. But what Swedenborg seems to be describing here are what we call "lucid dreams," dreams of an unusual clarity, in which the dreamer retains self-awareness.[39] The second vision is "with closed eye, which is as vivid as when the eyes are open, and like objects, even more beautiful and lovely, are offered to the sight." He adds that a similar vision can occur when the eyes are open, which suggests that he is speaking of something similar to what is called "eidetic imagery," the strange ability to see imaginary objects in startling clarity and detail. The *Encyclopaedia Britannica* describes "eidetic imagery" as "unusually vivid subjective visual phenomena." An eidetic object appears in minute photographic detail, and the person perceiving it behaves toward it as if it were really there. One famous eidetic person was the inventor Nikola Tesla, who could visualize an entire device "in his head," and use this as a blueprint for the actual construction. The phenomenon may not be limited to one sense: Mozart reportedly heard an entire piece of music before setting the notes to paper, suggesting he possessed a form of eidetic hearing.

In the third kind of sight, "the eyes are open, and the things in heaven, both spirits and other things, are represented." Swedenborg called this a "representative vision," and remarked that "it differs entirely from the ordinary imagination." It was, he said, very familiar to him, and one suspects that it was in this state that he saw heaven, hell and the other interior worlds. He also remarks that it is "rather obscure," which suggests that, as in any obscured sight, not everything may be seen correctly; in other words, Swedenborg may have been mistaken on occasion. Toksvig records an account by the Danish General Tuxen, who once came upon Swedenborg unexpectedly when he was in this state. Addressing Swedenborg, who had his "elbows on the table, his hands supporting his face . . . his eyes open and much elevated," the General saw him rise "with some confusion" and come toward him "in singular and visible uncertainty, expressed by his countenance and hands."[40] This description of Swedenborg awakening from a trance is reminiscent of Friedrich Rittelmeyer's account of Rudolf Steiner's behavior after "reading" the Akashic Record. Rittelmeyer, a Protestant pastor and one of Steiner's closest followers, writes that when people came to Steiner for spiritual advice, Steiner would sit where he could avoid looking into the light. He then lowered his eyes and made "a deliberate adjustment of his being." Afterward Rittelmeyer noticed that

> at the beginning of a conversation it was not easy for [Steiner] to find the right words. One said to oneself then that he had surely been occupied with his spiritual investigations and needed a few seconds for the transition to the world of purely physical existence. He tried to find the appropriate word, missed it, and stopped.[41]

In his brilliant and exhaustive study *Hypnagogia*, Andreas Mavromatis suggests that hypnagogic imagery is linked to the pre-cortical structures of the brain, such as the thalamus, hippocampus, medulla oblongata, and also the limbic system, mentioned earlier, in association with Swedenborg's peculiarly sensitive sense of smell. As language is a function of the neocortex, these structures are pre-verbal, and the shift from the old to the new brain can be disorienting; hence Steiner's fumbling for the "appropriate word" after "reading" the Akashic Record. This may also possibly account for Swedenborg's "uncertainty" upon being unexpectedly addressed by General Tuxen.

In the fourth sight Swedenborg seems to be describing a state in which he was completely removed from his body and had entered the spiritual worlds entirely, and could move and act within them. In this state, a man "is separated from the body and in the spirit, and the man then cannot at all know otherwise than that he is awake." He "enjoys all his senses, as that of touch, hearing and sight, and I have no doubt the other senses as well. It is a fuller sight than that of wakefulness, because more exquisite; and in that state one does not apperceive otherwise than that he is awake, except from the fact that he relapses into the wakefulness of the body."

When looking at Swedenborg's account, it is clear he is describing different levels of separation from the outer world and a deepening immersion in the inner one. The first occurs in sleep, a state in which we normally have visions, which we call dreams. The next occurs in our waking state, but with the eyes closed; it seems an unusual variety of imagination, and seems to be of individual objects, rather than of landscapes or entities like angels or spirits. The third takes place with the eyes open; now more is seen, but it is, as he says, "rather obscure," and there is still an awareness of the external world (this is a sight similar to the hypnagogic state). Here Swedenborg seems to be "outside" what he is seeing, as if he were watching it on a screen. In the last sight, the external world is left behind, and consciousness seems to float free of the body, now not only observing the spirit realms but actually entering them; we might want to call this an out-of-body experience, or an example of astral traveling or an unusually vivid lucid dream or some sort of spiritual virtual reality. In these states, Swedenborg seemed to have actually gone to heaven, hell or the intermediate world of spirits, in the way that the rest of us will go after our deaths.

We may want to argue that by definition, anyone who has visions of this sort is mad. But then we would be indicting the entire human race, as we all pass through the hypnagogic state at least twice a day, when falling asleep and when waking up. The difference is that most of us remember very little of what we see in these brief glimpses, and if we do, we consider it a weird dream and promptly forget about it. Swedenborg and many like him—Jung, Steiner, Van Dusen and others—were intrigued enough by this state to explore it. Steiner built an occult history of the world on what he saw; Jung developed a technique he called "active imagination," and used it as a means of psychological development. Swedenborg did something more radical, and in a way, simpler. He went to heaven and hell.

Chapter Four: Slayer of the Real

4

In this last chapter I would like to look at some aspects of what Swedenborg saw and experienced during his visits to heaven, hell and the intermediate realm he called the world of spirits. Much has been written about this, not the least by Swedenborg himself; more than anything else he accomplished, for more than two centuries now it is his cartography of the spiritual worlds that has attracted the interest of a number of brilliant individuals. Although Swedenborg himself saw his esoteric reading of Scripture as his true task—so important that it announced the revelation of the true meaning of Christianity—to modern readers, his biblical exegesis seems something of a magnificent eccentricity, a testament to his powers of concentration and application.

In Swedenborg's day, the Bible was still the central text in the Western canon, and every literate person was expected to be well versed in it. But Swedenborg himself may have recognized that an undiluted close reading of Scripture—specifically the books of Genesis, Exodus and Revelation—may have proved too daunting even for the most devout, and he decided to leaven his critical work with something akin to parables. These were the "inter-chapter material" that he included in his gargantuan *Arcana Coelistia* and other works, his accounts of how things were in heaven, hell, on other planets and in the spirit world. The bulk of his reports on heaven and hell were collected in a book of that name, and *Heaven and Hell* today remains the most popular of Swedenborg's many works. It is certainly the most readable, and if there is such a thing as an introduction to his ideas, this is it.

Today, if people ask me who Swedenborg was and I answer that he wrote books about his visits to heaven and hell, the usual response is a raised eyebrow, a nod and a facial expression suggesting that, in that case, he must have been crazy. In Swedenborg's day, however, the idea that one could journey to heaven and hell met with a different response. For most people, heaven and hell were real places, and although unusual, the idea that someone could travel there was not necessarily impossible.

For some the notion was blasphemous, for others not really startling, given all the other fantastic journeys and discoveries of recent times—science, we know, was just beginning, and there seemed no limit to what man could do. For a good number of people, however, it showed that the anonymous author of these otherworldly travelogues was clearly insane. Along with the accounts of his psychic abilities, to which we will come shortly, Swedenborg's depictions of his encounters with angels, spirits and the inhabitants of other worlds are what keep his name appearing in various books on the history of the occult and the paranormal.

In reaction to this, and in order to give more attention to his scientific and theological writings, some commentators have taken to playing down the occult aspect of Swedenborg's heavenly visions. For Lars Bergquist, Swedenborg was "characterized throughout his long life by a striking desire and ability to make his feelings concrete and human." Angels show him truths and regions of heaven. These beings, he wrote in *Conjugial Love*, are "affections of love in human form."[1] During a question-and-answer period at a talk on his biography of Swedenborg, Bergquist reinforced this opinion, answering a question about Swedenborg's angels by saying that Swedenborg had a great need to "give a face to his love." Looking at Swedenborg's writings, it is easy to see that something like this is true. His scientific work is full of very concrete images. He writes of the body's "pipes, ovens and little bladders," and how they "cooperate" with each other. There is the "gratework of the ribs," he talks of "old blood . . . clad in black garments and hurried away to the tombs of the liver." "Hungry veins . . . eagerly snatch" at gastric juices, and there are nerves that seem like "a married pair, the intercostals doing the husband's office and the par vagum the wife's."[2] Other similar concrete metaphors and similes fill his descriptions of the body's construction. For all his prolixity, Swedenborg was not an abstract thinker. His thinking is invariably pictorial.

The universe itself was in human form, the Grand Man, of which the many worlds and their inhabitants form the parts. Swedenborg indeed thought that seeing is believing: "Anything invisible," he wrote, "cannot be reduced to a concept one can think about."[3] One reason Swedenborg avoided argument—aside from his inhibition because of his stammer—may have been because he thought in images, not in premises and consequences, and you cannot argue with an image, you can only show it. So, when Swedenborg talked of angels, of the beautiful gardens of heaven, and of the sulfurous wastelands of hell, he was merely doing what he had always done: presenting his thought in graphic, almost tangible images.

But while it is clear that Swedenborg was a "concrete thinker," he also stated unequivocally that his journeys to heaven and hell actually took place. He had really gone there, and he had really "heard and seen." The fact that he spent hours at a time hovering in the twilight realm of the hypnagogic suggests that while there he was actually seeing something. Swedenborg's visits to heaven and hell were, I think, more than allegories of human weaknesses and divine grace. They were, I think, excursions into other states of consciousness, states that others also entered. It is true that the descriptions these others gave of their experiences differ from Swedenborg's. But in some essentials I think they are very similar, which suggests that the terrain they explored was much the same.

But before we journey with Swedenborg into other realms, it might be good to take a brief look at the accounts of his paranormal abilities.

Much has been written about these and, as I have mentioned, they turn up in practically every history of the occult. In Swedenborg's lifetime, they were the source of renown and, at times, notoriety. Yet rather than detract from his less sensational accomplishments, to me they only add to his interest and significance. In themselves, the kinds of powers Swedenborg exhibited are not particularly important; in many esoteric disciplines they are considered a by-product of spiritual development and, more often than not, the student is advised not to pursue them or to be distracted by them. Nor are they as rare as one might think. My own encounters with precognitive dreams, synchronicities, telepathy and other paranormal phenomena suggest that we need only pay close attention to our experience to detect the presence of some of these (and keeping a dream journal, as Swedenborg did, is a good way to do this). Most of us experience some form of the paranormal without even recognizing it, which suggests that rather than a special "gift" possessed by only the few, these powers are a part of human nature—submerged, yes, but still present and on occasion active. It is more than likely that their rarity is really only a result of our ignorance about them. It is also true that life in the modern world offers little use for them. Living in a culture that denies their existence and stigmatizes those who recognize them as frauds or superstitious fools, it is not surprising that we have come to be oblivious to them, or to ignore their presence when felt. Predictably, it is the philosophers, the men of intellect, who deny the reality of the paranormal, while the unlearned often accept it as a fact of life. As

Swedenborg knew, shepherds and children are more apt to see angels than are so-called "wise men."

This said, it has to be admitted that, if we go by most accounts, Swedenborg's powers were extraordinarily acute. They were considered so remarkable that, as we have seen, a philosopher of the stature of Kant thought them worthy of investigation. There are several stories of Swedenborg's powers, but three stand out as particularly impressive: the Stockholm fire, the Queen of Sweden's secret, and the lost receipt. The first is perhaps the best known. While at a dinner in Gothenburg upon his return to Sweden from England, Swedenborg got up suddenly and left the party, then returned looking pale and shaken. When asked what was wrong, he replied that a fire had just broken out in Stockholm, some 300 miles away. The fire had started on Södermalm, where his house was, and was spreading quickly. Swedenborg continued to be restless and uneasy, and soon announced that the house of a friend of his was already in ruins. His excitement continued, but by eight o'clock—two hours after he first spoke of it—he was relieved, and told the party that the fire had been extinguished just three houses before his. That evening the Governor was told of Swedenborg's vision, and the following morning Swedenborg was brought before him to be questioned. Swedenborg described the fire precisely, explaining how it had started, how long it burned, and how it had been stopped. News of his vision spread through the city, and many people were concerned for friends who might have been hurt. Swedenborg had had his vision on a Saturday; and Monday evening, a messenger arrived from Stockholm, sent by the Board of Trade. The letters he carried described the fire exactly as Swedenborg had, and this was confirmed the next day when the royal courier arrived at the Governor's, and again related the facts about the fire. It seemed that Swedenborg had seen the fire at exactly the same time as it occurred, as it had been stopped at eight o'clock, and this was the same time as when he had announced to his companions in Gothenburg that the danger had passed.

On another occasion, Swedenborg was at a court reception, and the Queen asked him many things about life in the spirit world—by this time his reputation as a seer was well known. She then asked somewhat skeptically if he had seen her deceased brother. Swedenborg said he had not, and the Queen asked him to see if he could make contact with him, and to give him her greeting. Swedenborg said he would. At the next reception, Swedenborg was again there, and he approached the Queen. He passed on a greeting to her from her brother, and also her brother's apologies for not answering her last letter. Swedenborg then said that her brother had asked him to answer it for him, and whispered something to the Queen. Shaken, the Queen replied, "No one but God knows this secret."

The third famous episode involves the widow of a Dutch ambassador who came to Swedenborg for help. She was being pressured for payment for a silver tea service, which she was certain her husband, who had recently died, had already paid. The problem was that she could not find the receipt. Could Swedenborg help? He said he would try.

A few days later, Swedenborg told the widow that he had spoken with her husband, who confirmed that the tea service had been paid for several months before his death, and that the receipt for it could be found in a bureau drawer. The widow told Swedenborg that she had already searched the bureau but could find nothing. Swedenborg then told her that the receipt was in a secret drawer, and that it was hidden there with other papers. After he informed her how to locate the compartment, the widow found it, and inside she discovered both the receipt and the other documents.

All three of these stories have been told in different ways, with slight changes in setting, but the gist remains the same. Swedenborg seems to have exhibited clear evidence for clairvoyance, and also for being able to speak with the dead. In one instance at least, he also seemed to have a precognitive ability, and in the last month of his life, predicted the exact date of his death. Discovering through the spirit world that John Wesley wished to meet him, he wrote to Wesley saying he would be happy to speak with him. Wesley wrote back saying that he was unfortunately unable to accept his invitation now as he was about to start on a speaking tour of the country, but would very much like to do so on his return to London. Swedenborg answered that sadly this would be impossible, as he was to die a month later, on the twenty-ninth of March, which he did. The information he gathered about the Queen's secret was obviously known to the Queen, so it could be accounted for by telepathy. But the location of the hidden bureau drawer was not known to anyone living at the time, so his acquiring it cannot be accounted for in that way. Unless we argue that in the case of the Queen and the silver tea service a conspiracy was involved—which seems highly unlikely—we are left with the fact that Swedenborg had somehow gained knowledge of these things from the dead.

Swedenborg often remarked, almost offhandedly, about his conversations with the famous dead. It was not unusual for him to comment casually, "As St. Paul said to me just the other day . . ." This sort of thing is, of course, not uncommon among spiritualists or "channellers," but it seems clear that Swedenborg did not do it to impress or to glean some importance from hobnobbing with ghostly celebrities. It was just a fact of his life. He also made it clear that he could not contact just anyone. When asked by the Queen if he could speak with everyone deceased, Swedenborg replied: "I cannot converse with all, but with such as I have known in this world; with all royalty and princely persons, with all renowned heroes, or great and learned men, whom I have known either personally or from their actions or writings; consequently of all of whom I could form an idea; for it may be supposed that a person whom I never knew or of whom I could form no idea I neither could nor would wish to speak with."

Curiously, another seer, whom I have had occasion to mention already, was also intimate with the dead. In the years prior to his becoming an esoteric teacher, Rudolf Steiner had two remarkable experiences involving the recently deceased. In both instances, however, he did not know the men himself, but came to know them through being in close contact with their surroundings, specifically their libraries. So intimate did his posthumous acquaintance with these men become that both families, one in Vienna, the other in Weimar, asked him to give the eulogy at the memorial services. Steiner claims that he was able to follow both men in the spirit world after their death, and this seems to be a case of his being able, like Swedenborg, to enter into a deep sympathy with the person: he could "form an idea" of them so rich that it allowed him to enter into their "spirit" quite literally. Something similar happened to Steiner when he met the philosopher Nietzsche, who clearly was not dead, but who had been insane for several years. Steiner knew Nietzsche intimately, through his writings, and when he was ushered into Nietzsche's company by the philosopher's sister, Steiner had a vivid vision of Nietzsche's "soul."[4] As much as any specifically psychic ability, it seems that being able to "speak with the dead" may also involve the ability to enter into a deep, imaginative rapport with them—and it is highly possible that the two are really only different ways of speaking about the same thing. And it may even be the case that if I enter into, say, Beethoven's "spirit" through my appreciation of his music and a study of his life, I am in as much contact with him as I would be if he spoke to me from the spirit world. More contact, in fact, as the essence of Beethoven—or of any artist or thinker—is in his work, and this, unlike his physical shell, outlasts his lifetime.

But although Swedenborg seemed to possess a remarkable facility for communicating with the dead, this was really only an adjunct to his main theme: the true meaning of Scripture, and the character of the spiritual realms.

*

Readers interested to know how Swedenborg understood the Bible can go to the source and enter the rewarding but difficult terrain of *Arcana Coelistia* themselves. Here I can only touch on the central insight that informs his exegesis: the theory of correspondences. For Swedenborg, the Bible is written in a symbolic code, and its purpose is to depict truths about the spiritual worlds. This code is one of correspondences. The truth about correspondences was known to the ancients, but for us, and for the people of Swedenborg's time, it is lost. Its essence is that there is a direct, one-to-one link between the elements of our world, both natural and man-made, and the spiritual worlds within. "The whole natural world," Swedenborg wrote, "corresponds to the spiritual world—not just the natural world in general, but actually in details."[5] "It is vital," he continues, "to understand that the natural world emerges and endures from the spiritual world, just like an effect from the cause that produces it."[6] The natural world for Swedenborg means "all the expanse under the sun, receiving warmth and light from it. All the entities that are maintained from this source belong to that world. The spiritual world, in contrast, is heaven. All the things that are in the heavens belong to that world."[7]

For Swedenborg, the entire physical world gains its being and existence from the spiritual one. In a sense, the world, our world, is a kind of reflection of the higher one. Or, to put it a different way, our world is a kind of book which, read rightly, can tell us things about the higher world. As Czeslaw Milosz put it, "Swedenborg's world is all language."[8] For Gertrude Stein, "A rose is a rose is a rose," but not for Swedenborg: it has a specific meaning in relation to his notion of conjugial love. Everything else in the world has a similar specific meaning as well. For Swedenborg, as for Goethe who came after him, "*Alles Vergängliche/Ist nur ein Gleichnis*," all that is transitory is but a symbol. A tree is not only a tree; it is a sign, or, better, a symbol, although for Swedenborg, who kept a very strict tally between the things of this world and their counterparts in the other, "sign" is perhaps the better word. An example is the sun's light and warmth; in the spiritual worlds, this corresponds to the Divine's truth and love. There are many other examples, and Swedenborg provides their details in, it has to be said, a rather dry, factual manner. But the idea is really not that foreign. We can perhaps grasp what Swedenborg is getting at if we think of the relation, say, between the expression on someone's face and what they are feeling. The expression is the physical sign of a spiritual—inner, psychological—reality. We can read someone's state from their expression, and if we are aware of the code, we can read the world and from it understand the truths of the spirit.

Although Swedenborg gave it a unique understanding, his notion of correspondences is not uncommon in the hermetic tradition. In fact, it is the central axiom of that tradition, the famous "As above, so below" attributed to the mythical founder of alchemy and magic,

Hermes Trismegistus. And although Swedenborg saw it as the key to the true meaning of the Bible, it has not had its greatest effect in that way. Elsewhere I have written about the enormous influence Swedenborg's notion of correspondences had on Symbolism, the most important artistic movement of the nineteenth century.[9] There I also point out that we are all familiar with the use of correspondence in our everyday language, although we do not see this as such. Metaphors are a form of correspondence, in the sense that they "stand for something else." If I say of someone that he had a "burning stare," I do not mean his gaze literally burned me; I mean that his stare was so intense that it was like being burned by it. The metaphor "burning" stands for the intensity of the stare. Purists may argue that this, and the French poet Charles Baudelaire's poetic use of correspondences—which is really a more vital use of metaphor—is a watering down of Swedenborg's intent. But it strikes me that, aside from students of Swedenborg's *Arcana Coelistia*, it is this form of correspondence that most of us have some experience of. But where Swedenborg's correspondences were strict associations between the things of this world and those of the spiritual realms, Baudelaire's use of the theme was looser, and tended to focus on correspondences between more sensual phenomena.

In his famous poem "Correspondances," Baudelaire tells us that "Nature is a temple," a "forest" through which we pass "symbolically," and in a few brief lines, he creates an atmosphere of shifting contours and dreamy surfaces, in which "perfumes and colors are mixed in strange profusions" inducing a sense of "the strange expansion of things infinite." Baudelaire's correspondences between perfumes and colors inaugurates the fascination with synaesthesia, the evocative blending of the senses that would dominate the aesthetics of the late nineteenth century—the most well-known example of this is Arthur Rimbaud's poem "Vowels," in which he associates specific colors with the vowels: A black, E white, I red, O blue, U green.[10] Symbolism was an aesthetic of suggestion, of hints and nuances, and the general effect of Symbolist art was to induce in its audience a sense of some vague "otherness" hovering behind the physical world, the feeling that there was something more, just out of reach, waiting to be found. For Symbolism, the objects of the material world are so many question marks, inviting us to peer beneath their surface and catch a glimpse of a deeper meaning. The Symbolist, as the critic Anna Balakian said, was intent on "deciphering . . . the enigmas of life."[11]

Swedenborg, however, was not a Symbolist, nor even a Romantic; he was a scientist and a man of the Enlightenment, and clarity and rigor were essential to him, not vague suggestion. For Swedenborg, the "symbols" laid before him in the natural world were not mere triggers for poetic musings; they were the alphabet of heaven. And the primer for learning that alphabet, and eventually how to read the words written in it, was his *Arcana Coelistia*.

The basic message to be found in these symbols was that everything in the world received its being from a higher world, from heaven. And to give his readers some idea exactly what that world was like,

Swedenborg provided something of a travelogue, a cross between a spiritual Rough Guide and a series of heavenly pantomimes, depicting the customs and mores of the divine and diabolical territories. The strangest thing about heaven and hell is that they are so like our own world. In heaven there are gardens, houses, rivers, flowers. Angels there eat, socialize and have sexual relations. The scenery is beautiful and inspiring. Hell, as you might expect, is a less pleasant place, full of squalid huts, tawdry brothels, dark streets where the inhabitants brawl and argue and nasty odors prevail. The difference between these realms and our more familiar earthly dwelling is that, here, while we may give lip service to the idea that our attitudes and choices create the kind of world we live in, in heaven and hell, this is literally and absolutely true. Although our limited earthly understanding must see heaven and hell as "places," in reality they are "states of mind." In a very real sense, heaven and hell exist within our own consciousness. We are not sent there after death via the will of a patriarchal deity. We arrive at our place in eternity through what Swedenborg called our "true affections," our real loves and affinities. And although we may deceive others and ourselves about these while on earth, when we enter the afterlife, this is not so.

One of the clearest expressions of the idea that heaven and hell are of our own making and that we are led there by our choices is not found, as one might expect, in one of Swedenborg's books, but in Bernard Shaw's "philosophical comedy" *Man and Superman*.[12] In the "Don Juan in Hell" section—often excluded from productions of the play—

John Tanner dreams that he is Don Juan and that he is languishing in hell. Hell, however, is not a place of torment and pain—although Tanner finds it such—but a place, as Shaw puts it, where "one has nothing to do but amuse oneself." And the company he finds himself in is not of criminals and cutthroats, but of "respectable" people. In hell, however, these "respectable" folk can relieve themselves of the pretense they maintained while alive, and their true inclinations can blossom. So they indulge in chitchat and gossip, take on the appearance that suits their vanity (self-love), compliment each other, and gratify their appetites for sensual delights. When a new guest, Donna Ana, arrives, she is surprised to discover that she is in hell; after all, she has led a life of sacrifice and propriety. When she insists that she does not belong there, the Devil informs her that she can leave for heaven at any time. Ana is stunned by this:

> *Ana*: But surely there is a great gulf fixed.
> *The Devil*: Dear lady: a parable must not be taken literally. The gulf is the difference between the angelic and the diabolical temperament. What more impassable gulf could you have?

The Devil continues with a long speech, in which, among other things, he informs Ana that, although they are generally regarded as "higher, more cultivated, poetic, intellectual, and ennobling" than a racecourse, most people prefer racing to classical concerts. Nothing prevents them from attending the concert except their taste, and the same is true of heaven. "A mere physical gulf they could bridge," he tells her. "But the gulf of dislike is impassable and eternal. And that is the only gulf that separates my friends here from those who are invidiously called the blest."

Tanner, too, wants to escape hell and get to heaven, where live "the masters of reality." Shaw's heaven, like Swedenborg's, is not a place of happiness but of work, what Shaw called life's "incessant aspiration to higher organization, wider, deeper, intenser self-consciousness, and clearer self-understanding." Hell is "the home of the unreal and of the seekers of happiness," Tanner declares. "It is the only refuge from heaven . . . and from earth, which is the home of the slaves of reality."[13] How far is this from Swedenborg's dictum that no one in heaven is idle? For Swedenborg, every angel has his "uses." In his heaven there are no cherubic choirs, strumming on harps. "Such a life would not be active," Swedenborg wrote, "but idle . . . there is no happiness in life apart from activity."[14] For those who think heaven is the place of their eternal rest, Swedenborg's account of it is sobering, to say the least.

The passage to heaven or hell lies through what Swedenborg called the world of spirits, an intermediate realm that roughly accords with the Purgatory of Catholicism. The world of spirits is rather like our own world, and the newly dead are often unaware of their transition, and linger on, still trying to gratify their carnal desires. Gradually the truth becomes clear, and the dead then come to terms with their true affections. Swedenborg writes, "the world of spirits is neither heaven nor hell. . . . It is where a person first arrives after death, being, after some time has passed, either raised into heaven or cast into hell, depending on his life in the world."[15] After confronting their true selves, the dead are "opened to their internals" and begin to drift to their rightful places. Human beings, Swedenborg said, possess two essential qualities or powers: intention and discernment, or love and reason. What is true about us is what we think from "intention" and really do, not merely what we "know." According to Swedenborg, "a person is a person by virtue of his intention and his resulting understanding, and not from understanding apart from intention."[16] In a very real way, for Swedenborg, it is the thought that counts.

It is impossible to deceive anyone in the spirit worlds, as by definition these worlds are states of being. On earth we may be able to say one thing and think another, but this is not so in the spirit world. There, you really are what you are. Appearance and being are identical. "Absolutely everyone there is resolved into a state in which he speaks the way he thinks, and displays in his expression and gestures what his intentions are."[17] We recall Swedenborg's sensitivity to hypocrisy and dissimulation. In the spirit world there is no avoiding the truth. What we really are depends on what we really feel. If our true affections show a real love for others and a desire to transcend the self, then, after a brief period, we begin to move toward heaven. But if our true affections center on self-love and all that entails—greed, envy, licentiousness, desire for power over others—then, regardless of appearances, we make our way to hell. It is surprising whom we would find there. "Why, the best people are here—princes of the church and all," says one inhabitant in Shaw's play.[18] Swedenborg himself often hobnobbed with bishops in the bad place.

And a bad place it is. Although, as Czeslaw Milosz points out, "Swedenborg's detailed descriptions of beautiful gardens, their trees and their flowers in Heaven, and of slums, dirt and ruins in Hell do not mean that he believed they existed other than in imagination," this "imagination" is "the most real existence."[19] For Swedenborg—and for Blake who came after him—this "other" world is more "real" than any physical "place," if only for the simple reason that any place we might physically go to has its roots in the imaginative realms. Swedenborg's heaven and hell exist in what the philosopher Henry Corbin calls the "imaginal," which is reached via what Corbin calls the "imaginative consciousness" or the "cognitive imagination."[20] But to say that hell exists in the imagination does not make it any less tangible, or, by Swedenborg's account, any less repellent.

*

Many readers otherwise open to Swedenborg's thought are put off by his accounts of hell. This includes figures like William Blake and R. W. Emerson. Blake's *The Marriage of Heaven and Hell* is a pointed criticism of Swedenborg's vision, which separates the two realms. Unlike Shaw, for Blake, Swedenborg's heaven is a very dull place, while Blake's own account of hell makes it attractive: angels are rather staid bores, but the devils are lively, vital characters.

Emerson, who called Swedenborg a "colossal soul" and "one of the mastodons of literature," also remarked apropos of Swedenborg's hell that "A vampire sits in the seat of the prophet and turns with gloomy appetite to images of pain."[21] It is not difficult to see why Emerson felt this. Swedenborg's hell is an unremittingly revolting state of being, a nightmarish blend of Hieronymus Bosch and some of William S. Burroughs's most paranoiac visions, and one cannot be censured for wondering if Swedenborg derived some gratification from knowing that the souls whose true affections brought them there deserved their fate. As in the case of Dante's *Inferno*, there is a hint of sadism in Swedenborg's account of the punishments inflicted on the damned, even if, as he maintained, punished and punisher are the same. Ordure, vomit, unspeakable stenches, insatiable desires, gnawing hungers, interminable darkness, the constant harangue of petty, bickering souls await hell's inmates. "In some hells," Swedenborg tells us, "one can see something like the rubble of homes or cities after a great fire. . . . In milder hells, one sees tumble-down huts, crowded together. . . . Within the houses are hellish spirits, constant brawls, hostilities, beatings. . . . There are robberies and hold-ups in the street. . . . In some hells there are nothing but brothels that look disgusting and are full of all kinds of filth and excrement."[22] (Even granting that street crime was far worse in Swedenborg's day than in ours, it is surprising how reminiscent this description is of much of our own modern cities.)

There are other hells too. Forests filled with dangerous beasts, dark dank caves, arid wastes and other equally undesirable places await those who belong there. These and all the other unappetizing landscapes are the result of the choices the hellish souls have made in life, and although Swedenborg's hell is unmistakably nasty, the damned suffer even more, if by chance the light of heaven falls on them. They belong in hell, and miss it if they are away from it. And in a sense, they existed there for some time before their deaths. Given that the hells Swedenborg describes are really reflections of the inner states of the souls who inhabit them, these unfortunates have carried their own, personal hell around with them for many years. And again, this is something we can find in our own experience. We all know what it is like to be consumed by envy, rage, lust, greed or any of the other hellish emotions. We know how easy it is to give way to these, and how difficult it is to resist them and our own justifications for them. To go to hell or not is a choice we make every day. Jean-Paul Sartre may have famously believed that "hell is other people," but Swedenborg knew better. Hell, he tells us, is ourselves.

This is true also of heaven, which, to go by Swedenborg's description, is a state of almost unimaginable fulfillment. A reader first coming to Swedenborg's account of heaven may find it difficult to see this: what first strikes us is the description of heavenly houses, gardens, parks and erotic relationships. Blake once complained that the accepted notion of heaven was of an "allegorical abode where existence hath never come," and one suspects that, having been a reader of Swedenborg, he knew better. Swedenborg's heaven is nothing if not substantial. It has the kind of corporality we find in some nineteenth- and early-twentieth-century accounts of the afterlife, when mediums assured bereaved parents or spouses that their loved ones were enjoying themselves amid a heavenly counterpart of their life on earth. In 1916, for instance, the scientist and paranormal investigator Sir Oliver Lodge published a book about his dead son. *Raymond or Life and Death* told its readers that "the other side" was not very different from our own world. There people wore white robes, could eat, smoke cigars, and even have a whisky and soda.[23] Other accounts painted a similar picture. It was Swedenborg's "concrete" vision of heaven that the theologians of his time railed against; and even for readers who are sympathetic to his ideas, accounts of angels sharing meals or fulfilling their domestic duties can seem a bit much to swallow. For many, these accounts of angelic homes, clothes and sexual activity seem a simpleminded transference of earthly life into a heavenly setting, where everything is just as it is here, only better. Others, however, see it differently. Given Swedenborg's description, the higher worlds seem not so "other," and as far as our own lives are directed toward the good and the true, we can participate in their significance while here on earth.

Yet the familiar setting afforded by Swedenborg's heaven is deceptive. There, things are not really the same as here. For one thing, time and space do not exist in heaven as they do on earth. Time there is not measured in days, weeks or years, but in changes in state. "Regardless of the fact that everything in heaven happens in sequence and progresses the way things do in the world," Swedenborg tells us, "still angels have no concept of time."[24] Time in our world is measured by the sun's apparent progress around the earth, producing what we know as the seasons. But in heaven, the sun is different. It does not produce days and years, but changes of state. Time is so alien to the angels that eternity for them does not imply an infinite time but an infinite state, the "timeless" condition described by mystics throughout the ages. Space is likewise absent in heaven. "In spite of the fact that everything in heaven seems to be in a place and in space just like things in the world," Swedenborg informs us, "angels have no concept or idea of place or space."[25] To travel in the spiritual world is accomplished by changes of state. "All journeys in the spiritual world occur by means of changes of state of more inward things."[26] "Being taken to worlds in space," Swedenborg says, "does not mean being taken or traveling in bodies, but in spirit. The spirit is guided through varying states of inner life, which appear to him like travels through space,"[27] a remark that sounds very similar to accounts of "spirit journeys" in shamanism. In heaven, distances are measured not by physical location but by degrees of empathy. Spirits of like mind are near each other in heaven, whatever their "location."[28] One beautiful way of expressing this is Swedenborg's claim that in heaven, no matter which way they turn, angels always face God, an insight that meant a great deal to the composer Arnold Schoenberg. In his unfinished oratorio *Jacob's Ladder*, Schoenberg, who came to Swedenborg via Balzac's novel *Seraphita*, has the angel Gabriel announce that: "Whether right, left, forward or backward, up or down—one has to go on without asking what lies before or behind us."

There are in fact three heavens: the celestial, the spiritual and the natural, each successively at a further distance from what Swedenborg calls "the Lord's Divine." Each participates to a greater or lesser degree in divine truth and love. Most ineffable is the celestial heaven, which participates directly in the will or intention of the Divine. The spiritual heaven participates in this less fully, but has an equal share of the divine understanding. The natural heaven, the lowest, has a small share in the divine discernment, and, by heavenly standards, very little of the divine intention. This arrangement makes clear that even in heaven, Swedenborg's notion of "degrees" holds sway. This gap between one heaven and another has real consequences; for instance, angels from one heaven cannot understand the language of those from the others, and if an angel from a lower heaven is brought into a higher one, the change in spiritual state is often too much to bear.

All of the heavens, and all of their many angels—who, we remember, are transformed human souls—come together to form the Grand Man, the vast image of the Universal Human, which makes up the body of the universe. The effect of reading Swedenborg's account of heaven is of something like a double exposure. There are the often pedestrian descriptions of "life in heaven," but through the reports of angelic "day-to-day" activities, one catches glimpses of a vibrant, complex, radiant world, a kind of supernal mosaic whose parts infinitely reflect each other. It is a cliché by now to say that Swedenborg's vision is on a par with Dante's; but if it is, it is nevertheless true.

I had read *Heaven and Hell* before, but what struck me in particular on this recent rereading, and on reading descriptions of heaven in other of Swedenborg's writings, especially the *Spiritual Diary*, was his accounts of the angels. In a fascinating essay, the philosopher Robert Avens defined an angel as "a human in whom the inner and the outer, the material and the spiritual, perfectly correspond to each other, that is, a person in a state of complete self-expression." Avens also spoke of Swedenborg's spiritual worlds. "Swedenborg's world of spirits and angels," he says, "is nothing more nor less than a further theophanic manifestation, an even more irresistible desire on the part of the Infinite to disperse itself in singular things so as to enable each thing to mirror the whole, to be a world."[29]

*

Reading of Swedenborg's angels made me think of other angels. There are, for example, the "terrifying angels" from the poet Rainer Maria Rilke's *Duino Elegies*. "Who, if I cried out, would hear me among the angels' hierarchies?" the poet asks. "Every angel is terrifying," Rilke tells us, and its "terror" is the exalted state in which it exists. In one of his best-known lines, Rilke tells us that "Beauty is nothing, but the beginning of terror, which we are still just able to endure," and Rilke's angels are beauty incarnate. If one pressed him against his heart, Rilke knows that he "would be consumed in that overwhelming existence."[30] Rilke's angels live in such superabundant being that "they do not know whether it is the living they are moving among, or the dead."[31]

A somewhat similar angel can be found in the Swiss novelist and playwright Friedrich Dürrenmatt's play *An Angel Comes to Babylon*. Here, the angel in question spends most of his time flying around the earth, marveling at its wonders. Like Rilke's angel, he is a symbol of pure affirmation. He assures one of the characters that all apparent disorders in the universe are only temporary glitches. "Heaven never lies. . . . Only sometimes it finds it difficult to make itself understood by humans. . . . All that is created is good, and all that is good, is happy. In my travels throughout creation, I have never encountered as much as one grain of unhappiness."

Another angel, perhaps more aware of life's tragedies, nevertheless exists in a similar transfigured state. In perhaps his most oft-quoted essay, the German-Jewish literary philosopher Walter Benjamin wrote of "the angel of history." The angel has his face turned toward the past, and where we humans can only perceive "a chain of events" he sees "one single catastrophe which keeps piling wreckage upon wreckage and hurls it in front of his feet." The angel, Benjamin tells us, would like to stay, "to awaken the dead, and make whole what has been smashed." But a "storm is blowing from Paradise," which "irresistibly propels him into the future."[32] Benjamin was inspired to write of his angel by a painting by Paul Klee, *Angelus Novus*—but even a passing mention of the many angels in Western painting would take us far from our subject.

As I read of Swedenborg's angels, I thought of these other super-beings, and reflected on Robert Avens's remark that angels are humans who have achieved "complete self-expression," which seems to suggest that the angelic state is one we can aspire to. I was also struck by one angelic characteristic in particular. Angelic speech, Swedenborg tells us, is utterly unlike that of humans. "Angels," he says, "can say more in a minute than many can say in half an hour. They can also set down in a few words the contents of many written pages."[33] "[A]ngelic language . . . has nothing in common with human language."[34] For one thing, "their speech is so full of wisdom that they with a single word can express things what men could not compass in a thousand words."[35] Given such a density of meaning, it is not surprising that retaining what has been gleaned from a conversation with angels may pose problems. "On occasion," Swedenborg tells us, "I have been assigned to the state in which angels were, and . . . have talked with them. At such times I understood everything. But when I was sent back into my earlier state . . . and wanted to recall what I had heard, I could not. For there were thousands of things that had no equivalent in concepts of natural thought, that were therefore inexpressible except simply through shiftings of a heavenly light—not at all by human words."[36]

Swedenborg says a great deal about angelic speech and angelic language: how when their thoughts are made "visible" they look like delicate waves; how the speech of celestial angels is like a gentle stream, but that of spiritual angels is energetic and distinct; how writing in the inmost heaven is made up of various curves and rounded forms; how the "good" is communicated through the vowels u, o and a, and the "true" in e and i; and also how, much like in the Kabbalah, angelic numbers reveal even more than their alphabet.[37] The idea that writing itself is somehow "magical" is old: the Egyptian god Thoth, later identified with the mythical Hermes Trismegistus, was the god both of magic and of writing, and both Kabbalists and philosophers like Martin Heidegger find in language itself the key to Being (*Dasein*). But what struck me most forcefully was Swedenborg's admission that, after returning to earth from heaven, he was unable to remember what the angels had told him. Clearly this was because of the terrific amount of meaning the angels can infuse into their utterances.

Now, it is not uncommon for people who have had mystical experiences to speak of them as ineffable. The reason for this is usually explained by saying that the experience itself is supernatural, divine or somehow beyond human reason. But there are other accounts of mystical experience that offer a different view. Two in particular came to mind as I was reading Swedenborg's account of angelic speech, and I would like to end this essay by relating these accounts to what Swedenborg has to say about the language of angels. For me, this seems to hold a key to unlocking the mysteries of mystical experience.

*

In an essay called "A Suggestion about Mysticism," the philosopher William James recounts his own experiences of "mystical states." "In one instance," James writes,

> I was engaged in conversation, but I doubt whether my interlocutor noticed my abstraction. What happened each time was that I

> seemed all at once to be reminded of a past experience; and this reminiscence, ere I could conceive or name it distinctly, developed into something further that belonged with it, this in turn into something further still, and so on, until the process faded out, leaving me amazed at the sudden vision of increasing ranges of distant facts of which I could give no articulate account. The mode of consciousness was perceptual, not conceptual—the field expanding so fast that there seemed no time for conception or identification to get in its work. There was a strongly exciting sense that my knowledge of past (or present?) reality was enlarging pulse by pulse, but so rapidly that my intellectual processes could not keep up the pace. The content was thus lost entirely to introspection—it sank into the limbo into which dreams vanish when we awake. The feeling—I will not call it belief—that I had had a sudden opening, had seen through a window, as it were, into distant realities that incomprehensibly belonged with my own life, was so acute that I cannot shake it off today.

The key phrase here is "the sudden vision of increasing ranges of distant facts of which I could give no articulate account," which strikes me as practically identical to what Swedenborg remarked about angelic speech, how it can contain "thousands of things that had no equivalent in concepts of natural thought, that were therefore inexpressible." The content of James's experience was not ineffable; the problem was that the connections he was making and the insights he was seeing ("The mode of consciousness was perceptual") came at such an incredible speed that his mind could not keep up with them.

On another occasion, James tried to salvage something of what he saw when under the influence of nitrous oxide. After speaking of the "immense emotional sense of reconciliation" that inhalation of the gas produced, James remarked on the central truth the experience afforded: "that every opposition, among whatsoever things, vanishes in a higher unity in which it is based, that all contradictions, so-called, are of a common kind, that unbroken continuity is of the essence of being; and that we are literally in the midst of an infinite, to perceive the existence of which is the utmost we can attain." In order to fix this insight in his consciousness, James made some notes. Yet when he went to look at these later, he was baffled by what he wrote. "What's mistake but a kind of take? What's nausea but a kind of –ausea? Sober, drunk, -unk, astonishment . . . Emotion—motion . . . It escapes, it escapes! But—what escapes, WHAT escapes." and so on, until James arrived at the summation of his revelation: "There are no differences but differences of degree between different differences of degree and no difference."[38]

James recognized that in mystical states, consciousness experiences "a tremendously exciting sense of an intense metaphysical illumination," in which "truth lies open to the view in depth beneath depth of almost blinding evidence." The problem was how to capture this evidence in words.

Another philosopher who followed James in the use of nitrous oxide to produce mystical states was P. D. Ouspensky. In a chapter called

"Experimental Mysticism" in his book *A New Model of the Universe*, Ouspensky describes his own attempts at trying to make sense of the altered state of consciousness provided by the gas.

Under nitrous oxide, Ouspensky found himself "in a world entirely new and entirely unknown," a world which "had nothing in common with the world in which we live." Like James, Ouspensky experienced the essential unity of existence. He saw that "everything is unified, everything is linked together, everything is explained by something else and in turn explains another thing. There is nothing separate, that is, nothing that can be named or described separately."[39] This inability to describe anything separately became clear to Ouspensky when he tried to explain to a friend what he was experiencing. "When I tried having someone near me during these experiments," Ouspensky wrote, "I found that no kind of conversation could be carried on."

> I began to say something, but between the first and second words of my sentence such an enormous number of ideas occurred to me and passed before me, that the two words were so widely separated as to make it impossible to find any connection between them. And the third word I usually forgot before it was pronounced, and in trying to recall it I found a million new ideas, but completely forgot where I had begun.[40]

Like James, Ouspensky too tried to find some way to recall some of the insights that flooded his consciousness. He writes that

> in a particularly vividly-expressed new state [. . .] when I understood very clearly all I wished to understand, I decided to find some formula, some key, which I should be able to, so to speak, throw across to myself for the next day [. . .] I found this formula and wrote it down with a pencil on a piece of paper.
>
> On the following day I read the sentence: "Think in other categories." These were the words, but what was their meaning?[41]

On another occasion, Ouspensky found himself formulating another enigmatic clue to the strange world he had entered. Sitting on a sofa smoking a cigarette, he glanced at his ashtray. "Suddenly," he writes, "I felt that I was beginning to understand what the ashtray was, and at the same time, with a certain wonder and almost with fear, I felt that I had never understood it before and that we do not understand the simplest things around us." Ouspenky's ashtray "roused a whirlwind of thoughts and images." It "contained such an infinite number of facts, of events; it was linked with such an immense number of things." Everything connected with smoking and tobacco "roused thousands of images, pictures, memories." Then the ashtray: how had it come into being? And the materials of which it was made? How had copper been discovered? What processes had it undergone, what treatment had it been subject to, how was it transported, who had done the work of transforming the raw material into the object on his table? These and dozens of other questions concerning the ashtray raced through his mind, and again Ouspensky tried to capture some of this in words.

But the next day, when he read what he had written, the insight had vanished. What had Ouspensky written? "A man can go mad from one ashtray." By this he had tried to convey the insight that "in one ashtray it was possible to know *all*."[42]

In their mystical states, both Ouspensky and James, like Swedenborg, had entered a world in which time and space as we usually understand them no longer existed, and in which the dominant insight was one of unity. It was also a world in which our usual categories of "subjective" and "objective" were transformed. Ouspensky writes that "In the new state all this was completely upset. . . . Here I saw that the objective and subjective could change places. The one could become the other . . . every thought, every feeling, every image was immediately objectified in real substantial forms which differed in no way from the forms of objective phenomena; and at the same time objective phenomena somehow disappeared, lost all reality, appeared entirely subjective, fictitious, invented, having no real existence."[43]

That "every thought, every feeling, every image was immediately objectified in real substantial forms" strikes me as very similar to Swedenborg's contention that heaven and hell are visual projections of our inner states. And that the "objective" world around us is really a "fiction," created by our current state of consciousness, seems an equally Swedenborgian insight.

It would not be difficult to draw comparisons between Swedenborg's description of conditions in heaven, and other accounts of higher consciousness. What strikes me as important here is that the difficulty

Swedenborg had in retaining the significance of his angelic conversations did not necessarily lie in what those conversations were about, but in the slowness of our intellects and, perhaps more important, the inefficiency of our language, something that Swedenborg clearly recognized and experienced. If angels can say more in a minute than we can in a half hour, and if they can convey more in a few words than we can in whole books, this must be because they have a language capable of doing this. But what they are saying is not necessarily ineffable. William James suggested that mystical states were simply an enlargement of our current state of consciousness, and this is supported by his remark that what he saw during his mystical experiences were "increasing ranges of distant *facts*" (my italics). This was also true of Ouspensky. His ashtray was an ordinary ashtray, but in his altered state he saw at once everything involved in it. There is nothing mystical about the fact that the copper had to be mined and that it had to go through several processes before it could appear on his table as an ashtray. What had happened was that he no longer took the ashtray for granted, and in his altered state recognized all it was connected to. And this was true of everything else he saw. The mystical state, it seems to me, is one in which facts that we normally blank out become vividly present, and the "ineffability" of these states is caused by the inability of our present language to accommodate this new information.

What James and Ouspensky experienced under nitrous oxide, and what Swedenborg perceived during his journeys to heaven, is that reality is infinitely more complex than we suspect, and seems to resemble something along the lines of the holographic model discussed earlier. And this seems to be reflected in Robert Avens's remark that "Swedenborg's world of spirits and angels" is an expression of the "irresistible desire on the part of the Infinite to disperse itself in singular things so as to enable each thing to mirror the whole, to be a 'world.'" If we remember that every part of a hologram contains the whole of it, just as Ouspensky's ashtray contained all, we can begin to see how the sudden revelation of this truth could prove overwhelming. According to Swedenborg, angels seem not to have this problem, and exist in a state in which the infinite unity of things is perpetually present to them. Hence our difficulty in understanding them. But if Robert Avens is right, and an angel is a human being who has achieved "complete self-expression," it may be possible, then, that at some point we too will share in this state. And the accounts handed down to us by people like Ouspensky, William James, Swedenborg and others suggest that they are not as uncommon or unobtainable as we might think.

Swedenborg, however, did not offer any advice as to how this might happen. He did not leave any instructions so that others could come to hear the angels speak, and more or less asked his readers to take his word on the subject, and even warned them against trying to follow the path he had taken. We can accept or reject this advice as we choose. My own inclination is to disregard the warning. Having discovered Swedenborg, I am now inclined to follow him on that journey within and to find out just how much I can see and hear for myself.

Endnotes

Introduction

1 See my *Turn Off Your Mind: The Mystic Sixties and the Dark Side of the Age of Aquarius* (New York: The Disinformation Company, 2003) and *A Secret History of Consciousness* (Great Barrington, MA: Lindisfarne, 2003).

2 Sadly, "the occult" is in many ways an inadequate term, covering in the popular mind a variety of disparate material ranging from mystical experience and the paranormal to UFOs and Satanism, which nevertheless share, as Wittgenstein called it, a "family resemblance." More accurately, the term designates a body of ideas about the cosmos and man's place within it and the literature dealing with them, which may have had its start in the early Gnostic tracts and the writings ascribed to Hermes Trismegistus circa A.D. 200, although some writers suggest an earlier origin. Space, however, doesn't allow me to do more than merely mention this. In its simplest sense, "occult" means "hidden" or "unseen."

3 Gary Lachman, "Heavens and Hells: the Inner Worlds of Emanuel Swedenborg," in *Gnosis*, Summer 1995; repr. in *Studia Swedenborgiana*,

October 1995; also repr. in Jay Kinney (ed.), *The Inner West* (New York: Jeremy P. Tarcher and Penguin, 2004).

[4] See Signe Toksvig, *Emanuel Swedenborg, Scientist and Mystic* (London: Faber and Faber, 1948), p. 373 n. 14.

[5] To do Kant justice, it should be recognized that this radical constraint on what we can know was prompted by his reaction to the radical skepticism of David Hume, who questioned the whole possibility of knowledge. In saying that such things as God, freedom, truth, etc. were not objects of knowledge, Kant was saying that they are things which we do not *experience*, at least not through the senses. We can and do, however, conceptualize these things, and one aim of Kant's difficult philosophy is to secure a sound foundation for knowledge and morality in Reason, in a time when their basis in revealed religion was dissolving.

[6] Again, this is an attribute he shares with Rudolf Steiner, who, like Swedenborg, was an eminently "practical mystic." Along with his philosophical and spiritual efforts, Steiner was an unusually successful educationalist, architect, stage director and agriculturalist, among other pursuits. Another esoteric teacher with a practical turn was the Russian-Armenian G. I. Gurdjieff. Like Swedenborg, Gurdjieff was extremely "handy," able to learn quickly and, often, to improve on, techniques for a variety of skills, from carpet weaving to cooking.

[7] Here Swedenborg is reminiscent of some other later "practical mystics": Goethe was a statesman, the poet Novalis was, like Swedenborg, an assessor of mines, and another poet, who was also a great reader of Swedenborg, O. V. de Lubicz Milosz, was a Lithuanian diplomat and a delegate to the League of Nations.

[8] For a full account of this intriguing notion, see Schuchard's articles "Yeats and the Unknown Superiors: Swedenborg, Falk and Cagliostro," in *The*

Hermetic Journal, no. 37, Autumn 1987; "The Secret Masonic History of Blake's Swedenborg Society," in *Blake, an Illustrated Quarterly*, vol. 26, no. 2, Fall 1992; "Swedenborg, Jacobites and Freemasonry," in Erland J. Brock (ed.), *Swedenborg and His Influence* (Bryn Athyn, PA: Academy of the New Church, 1988). See also her recent book *Why Mrs. Blake Cried* (London: Century, 2006).

[9] For an idea of how important a "true" reading of the Bible was to Newton, see David S. Katz, *The Occult Tradition from the Renaissance to the Present Day* (London: Jonathan Cape, 2005).

[10] Several books have been written about Swedenborg's life and work. Here I will list the ones I have consulted for this essay, and which I have found most useful: Signe Toksvig, *Emanuel Swedenborg, Scientist and Mystic* (London: Faber and Faber, 1948); Wilson Van Dusen, *The Presence of Other Worlds* (New York: Harper and Row, 1974); and Lars Bergquist, *Swedenborg's Secret* (London: Swedenborg Society, 2005).

[11] The fullest account of Swedenborg's life and times is Bergquist's *Swedenborg's Secret*. Signe Toksvig's biography, although lacking some of the detail that became available after her book was written, remains the most readable.

Chapter One

[1] Swedenborg, *The Spiritual Diary*, ed. Stephen McNeilly, tr. A. Acton (vol. I), G. Bush and J. H. Smithson (vols. II-III), G. Bush and J. F. Buss (vol. IV), J. F. Buss (vol. V), 5 vols. (London: Swedenborg Society, 2002–).

[2] Swedenborg, *Journal of Dreams 1743–1744*, tr. J. J. G. Wilkinson, ed. William R. Woofenden, intro. Wilson Van Dusen (London and Bryn Athyn, PA: Swedenborg Society and Swedenborg Scientific Association, 1989), p. 39.

[3] Ibid., p. 54.

[4] Toksvig, *Emanuel Swedenborg, Scientist and Mystic*, p. 14.

[5] Ibid., p. 20.

[6] Bergquist, *Swedenborg's Secret*, p. 1.

[7] Ibid., p. 5.

[8] I asked Lars Bergquist about this at a party celebrating the UK publication of his book. He agreed that his view of Jesper Swedberg differed considerably from Toksvig's earlier account, yet he offered no answer as to how, given they were writing about the same person, their accounts could be so conflicting.

[9] Toksvig, p. 14.

[10] Ibid.

[11] Swedenborg wasn't alone in recognizing the dangers of self-love. In his later teaching, the Armenian-Russian esoteric teacher G. I. Gurdjieff made Madame Vanity and Monsieur Self-Love the targets of unflinching self-observation.

[12] A younger brother, Daniel, died when Swedenborg was three.

[13] Swedenborg, *Conjugial Love*, tr. John Chadwick (London: Swedenborg Society, 1996), §395.

[14] Quoted in Bergquist, p. 294.

[15] Michael Stanley, "Introduction," in *Emanuel Swedenborg: Essential Readings* (Berkeley, CA: North Atlantic Books, 2003), p. 18.

[16] Aldous Huxley, *The Doors of Perception* and *Heaven and Hell* (St. Albans: Panther Books, 1977), p. 112. Huxley agreed with the idea, first presented by the philosopher Henri Bergson, that the brain, rather than being a *producer* of consciousness—in the way that, say, the liver produces spleen, an analogy first put forth by the eighteenth-century French physiologist Cabanis—acted instead as a kind of reducing

valve, or receiver, *limiting* the amount of information available to consciousness at a given moment. In this view, "each person," as the philosopher C. D. Broad writes, whom Huxley quotes, "is capable of remembering all that has ever happened to him and of perceiving everything that is happening everywhere in the universe." Yet, in order not to be overwhelmed, we need to eliminate the vast majority of this "largely useless and irrelevant knowledge" in order to focus on the "very small and special selection which is likely to be practically useful." Ibid., p. 19. Huxley argues that the effect of substances like mescaline or LSD—or of non-drug methods of altering consciousness—is to "open" this reducing valve, and so let in more of the information (i.e., reality) that we are "normally" unaware of. Certain individuals are able to achieve this "opening" more easily than the rest of us; among others, Huxley mentions specifically Swedenborg and Blake, borrowing from the former the title of perhaps his most famous book. The virtue of this is that, while our "normal" consciousness allows us to function quite well, it also produces a severely limited world, the kind of world perceived via the "measly trickle of the kind of consciousness which will help us to stay alive on the surface of this particular planet." Ibid., p. 20. The result is the radically utilitarian view of reality that dominates our actions, and the debilitating alienation from the world that is the common characteristic of modern consciousness. A reducing valve somewhat more open would show us, as Blake says, a reality "as it is, infinite." There is a danger, however, in a too effective elimination of the "reducing valve": the effect of mind-altering substances on the unprepared are well known. One also recalls the fate of the central character of Jorge Luis Borges's (himself a reader of Swedenborg) story "Funes the Memorious." Borges depicts the paralyzing effect of a consciousness unremittingly aware of "all that has ever happened to him" and of "everything that is happening everywhere in the universe."

[17] Swedenborg, *The Spiritual Diary*, vol. II, §§1584, 1585.

[18] A still-excellent summary of MacLean's model can be found in Arthur Koestler's classic *The Ghost in the Machine* (New York: Macmillan, 1967).

[19] Lyall Watson, *Jacobson's Organ* (London: Allen Lane, 1999), pp. 134–5. Along with a heightened sense of smell, people suffering from schizophrenia, Watson writes, often possess a particular odor; many psychiatrists become so attuned to this that they are able to gauge a patient's state of mind on a particular day by their smell. I have been unable to find any material suggesting that Swedenborg had an unusual or particularly strong body odor. Then again, in a time when standards of personal hygiene were less rigorous than our own, any peculiarities in Swedenborg's own smell would have been difficult to detect.

[20] Also known as the vomeronasal organ. Jacobson discovered the organ in 1809, and two years later published a paper on it.

[21] Toksvig, p. 34.

[22] Swedenborg, *The Spiritual Diary*, vol. I, §397.

[23] Not the society of the same name founded in 1875 by Helena Petrovna Blavatsky and Colonel Henry Steel Olcott in New York City.

[24] Harvey F. Bellin, " 'Opposition Is True Friendship': Swedenborg's Influence on William Blake," in Robin Larsen (ed.), *Emanuel Swedenborg: A Continuing Vision* (New York: Swedenborg Foundation, 1988), p. 92.

[25] Joscelyn Godwin, *The Theosophical Enlightenment* (Albany: SUNY Press, 1994), p. 100.

[26] Bergquist, pp. 169–70.

[27] For more on Count Zinzendorf, the Moravians, and Rabbi Falk, see my *Politics and the Occult* (Wheaton: Quest Books, 2008), pp. 53–65.

[28] Toksvig, pp. 57–8.

[29] For a history of automata see Gaby Wood's *Living Dolls* (London: Faber and Faber, 2002) and Tom Standage's *The Mechanical Turk* (London: Allen Lane, 2002). Victoria Nelson's excellent *The Secret Life of Puppets* (Cambridge, MA: Harvard University Press, 2001) looks at automata and related subjects from the perspective of the esoteric tradition.

[30] Toksvig, pp. 77–8.

[31] According, once again, to Marsha Keith Schuchard, Count Gyllenborg, Elizabeth's husband, was one of the people with whom Swedenborg was involved in the plot to restore the Stuarts.

[32] Swedenborg, *Conjugial Love*, §450.

Chapter Two

[1] W. R. Woofenden, "Swedenborg: The Man Who Had to Publish," in Larsen (ed.), *Emanuel Swedenborg: A Continuing Vision*, p. 308.

[2] Ibid.

[3] Nicholas Humphrey, *Soul Searching: Human Nature and Supernatural Belief* (London: Chatto & Windus, 1995).

[4] Francis Crick, *The Astonishing Hypothesis: The Scientific Search for the Soul* (London: Simon & Schuster, 1994), p. 3. For more on the urge to "explain consciousness," see the Introduction to my *A Secret History of Consciousness*.

[5] A formula repeatedly voiced by the philosopher John Searle.

[6] Swedenborg, *The Principia*, quoted in Steve Koke, "The Search for a Religious Cosmology," in Larsen (ed.), *Emanuel Swedenborg: A Continuing Vision*, p. 459.

[7] Swedenborg, *The Economy of the Animal Kingdom*, quoted in Toksvig, p. 2.

[8] Wilson Van Dusen, *The Presence of Other Worlds*, p. 22.

[9] David Bohm, *Wholeness and the Implicate Order* (London: Routledge & Kegan Paul, 1980). For a less technical exposition of Bohm's ideas, see David Bohm and F. David Peat, *Science, Order and Creativity* (New York: Bantam Books, 1987).

[10] Bohm's vision, though couched in the language of particle physics, is in many ways a re-formation of Gnostic and Kabbalistic ideas about the non-manifest reality underlying our spatial-temporal world. Gnostic writings speak of the *Pleroma*, Kabbalah of the *Ain Soph*, and later hermetic thinkers like Jacob Boehme of the *Ungrund* or "Abyss." All point to a kind of fundamental non-manifest unity out of which our universe of space and time emerges. Although Swedenborg's articulation of this idea differs from these, it is in its essentials very similar.

[11] This is again similar to the Kabbalistic scheme, in which the un-manifest *Ain Soph* or "Limitless Light" is drawn together into a point, *Kether*, the first of the ten *Sephiroth* or "vessels" that form the visible universe.

[12] See Koke, "The Search for a Religious Cosmology," p. 460.

[13] For the classic exposition of this, see Arthur O. Lovejoy, *The Great Chain of Being* (Cambridge, MA: Harvard University Press, 1936).

[14] P. D. Ouspensky, *In Search of the Miraculous* (London: Routledge & Kegan Paul, 1983), pp. 82–6.

[15] Arthur Koestler, *The Ghost in the Machine* (New York: Macmillan, 1968), pp. 45–58.

[16] Although an individual word has a "meaning," in the sense that it has a definition, in the context of a sentence, a word receives a greater meaning from the sentence as a whole. Likewise, while a sentence by definition

must mean something—otherwise it is a fragment or "incomplete sentence"—it conveys a greater meaning when understood as a part of a larger whole, say an essay or novel. "Rain" means precipitation in the form of drops of water. But it can also mean a ruined picnic, a much-needed drink for a thirsty garden, or a bothersome leak in the attic, given the context.

[17] Astronomy seems to be a study in which intuition plays a profound part. For an account of how our modern picture of the universe was arrived at almost unconsciously, see Arthur Koestler's very readable *The Sleepwalkers* (New York: Penguin, 1990). Another good reference is Colin Wilson's *Starseekers* (London: Panther, 1982). Along with other accounts, Wilson points out how Edgar Allan Poe's metaphysical prose poem *Eureka* (London: Hesperus Press, 2002), an utter failure in Poe's lifetime, anticipates several fairly recent cosmological "discoveries," including black holes.

[18] John D. Barrow and Frank J. Tipler, *The Anthropic Cosmological Principle* (Oxford: Clarendon, 1985).

[19] See John Gribbin and Martin Rees, *Cosmic Coincidences* (London: Black Swan, 1991).

[20] P. D. Ouspensky, *Tertium Organum* (London: Routledge & Kegan Paul, 1981), pp. 138, 289.

[21] Michael Stanley, "Introduction," in *Swedenborg: Essential Readings*, pp. 18–19.

[22] Stan Gooch, *The Paranormal* (London: Fontana, 1979), p. 242. See also Gooch's *Guardians of the Ancient Wisdom* (London: Fontana, 1980), pp. 100–1.

[23] I am aware of the evidence for "feeling" and "emotion" in plants, as I am for that suggesting forms of rational thought in some higher

primates. Important and instructive as these findings are, I don't think they alter in any significant way the main outlines of the plan given here. I am also aware that many people possessing "controlling egos" fail or choose not to use them, and prefer living in ways associated with lower rungs on the evolutionary ladder. We speak of "couch potatoes" and "party animals," and many plants and animals seem to lead nobler lives than these types. Yet the fact that some people do not actualize the potentials of their humanity does not support the argument that such potential does not exist.

[24] Another way to look at this scheme is like this: our senses tell us *that* something is; our intellect tells us what it is; our *animus* tells us if we like it or not; and our *anima* tells us what meaning, if any, it has for us, whether we should embrace it or avoid it.

Chapter Three

[1] See *The Grand Tour of William Beckford*, comp. and ed. Elizabeth Mavor (Harmondsworth: Penguin, 1986).

[2] Quoted in Toksvig, pp. 86–7.

[3] See Stephen Larsen's "Swedenborg and the Visionary Tradition," in Robin Larsen (ed.), *Emanuel Swedenborg: A Continuing Vision*, pp. 185–206.

[4] Swedenborg, *Journal of Dreams*, p. 5.

[5] Ibid., p. 49.

[6] Ibid., p. 103. Italics in the original.

[7] Ibid., p. 104.

[8] Ibid., p. 66.

[9] Ibid., p. 9.

[10] Ibid., p. 8.

[11] Ibid., pp. 12, 18.

[12] Wilson Van Dusen, "Swedenborg's Journey Within," ibid., p. xxxi.

[13] Swedenborg, *Journal of Dreams*, p. 7.

[14] We should note the emphasis on imbalance. Left-brain consciousness is not a "villain"; it is absolutely necessary and a completely "right-brain" consciousness would be undesirable. What is needed is the "just right" balance between the two, something that I have elsewhere called "the Goldilocks effect."

[15] Not all expressions of this resistance are of equal value, and I group different ones together in order to show how widespread and enduring the resistance is. An excellent account of how a lopsided valuation of science as the sole arbiter of truth in the last few centuries has resulted in our current malaise of meaninglessness can be found in Czeslaw Milosz's introduction to the work of his uncle and fellow Swedenborgian, O. V. de Lubicz Milosz, in *The Noble Traveller: The Life and Writings of O. V. de L Milosz*, ed. Christopher Bamford (West Stockbridge, MA: Lindisfarne, 1985).

[16] For the notion of subjectivity and the idea of a participatory consciousness, see my sections on Owen Barfield in *A Secret History of Consciousness*.

[17] William James, *The Varieties of Religious Experience* (New York: Collier Books, 1977), p. 119. James himself was no stranger to the sufferings of a "sick soul." In his early years he experienced periods of almost paralyzing depression and neurasthenia and, under the guise of a "communication from a French correspondent," he shared one of the most devastating attacks with the readers of *The Varieties*: "Whilst in this state of philosophic pessimism and general depression of spirits . . . I went one evening in a dressing-room in the twilight to procure some article . . . when suddenly there fell upon me without warning, just as if it came out of the darkness,

a horrible fear of my own existence. Simultaneously there arose in my mind the image of an epileptic patient whom I had seen in the asylum, a black-haired youth with greenish skin, entirely idiotic, who used to sit all day on one of the benches . . . with his knees drawn up against his chin, and the coarse gray undershirt, which was his only garment, drawn over them inclosing his entire figure. . . . This image and my fear entered into a species of combination with each other. *That shape am I*, I felt, potentially. Nothing that I possess can defend me against that fate, if the hour for it should strike for me as it struck for him. . . . I awoke morning after morning with a horrible dread at the pit of my stomach, and with a sense of the insecurity of life that I never knew before . . ." p. 138. James's existential dread is similar to his father's, Henry James, Sr.'s, "vastation": "One day . . . toward the close of May, having eaten a comfortable dinner, I remained sitting at the table, after the family had dispersed, idly gazing at the embers in the grate, thinking of nothing, and feeling only the exhilaration incident to a good digestion, when suddenly—in a lightning flash as it were—'fear came upon me, and trembling, which made all my bones to shake.' To all appearances it was a perfectly insane and abject terror, without ostensible cause, and only to be accounted for, to my perplexed imagination, by some damned shape squatting invisibly to me within the precincts of the room, and raying out from its fetid personality influences fatal to life." Quoted in *The Writings of William James*, ed. John J McDermott (New York: The Modern Library, 1968), p. 3. Both William's and Henry, Sr.'s, accounts play a central part in Colin Wilson's study of modern alienation, *The Outsider*. Henry James, Sr., called his experience a "vastation," taking the term from Swedenborg, who used it to characterize the emptying out of the ego, prior to receiving the influx from the Divine. Wilson refers to "vastation" frequently in his "Outsider cycle," using it to indicate the experience of absolute meaninglessness that must be faced before his Outsiders can begin the work of creative reconstruction: " 'vastation,' in one form or another, is an experience common to most Outsiders." *The Outsider* (Boston: Houghton Mifflin Co., 1956), p. 112. Wilson's Outsiders are individuals who, rejecting the spiritual bankruptcy of the modern age, are driven by a need for inner freedom. Henry James, Sr., recovered from his "vastation" through reading Swedenborg; William James overcame his depression through his belief in free will: "My first act of free will shall be to believe in free will." *The Writings of William James*, p. 7.

[18] Quoted in Toksvig, pp. 134–5.

[19] Swedenborg, *Journal of Dreams*, p. 21.

[20] Ibid., p. 20.

[21] Ibid., p. 17.

[22] The presence of winds, as in a great storm, seems common in "psychic" experience. In his account of his first attendance at a séance, the psychologist Stan Gooch writes that: "We . . . sang one of the simple Spiritualist hymns, and the presiding medium gave a short prayer. . . . At this point I became aware of a certain light-headedness. And then suddenly it seemed to me that a great wind was rushing through the room. In my ears was the deafening sound of roaring waters. Together these elements seized me and carried me irresistibly forward." *The Paranormal*, p. 16.

[23] Swedenborg, *Journal of Dreams*, p. 22: "Then, at the time I was prostrated, at that very moment I was wide awake, and saw that I was cast down." This seems to suggest that Swedenborg was somehow "looking" at himself as he lay on the floor.

[24] Ibid., pp. 22–3.

[25] Wilson Van Dusen, *The Presence of Other Worlds*, p. 45.

[26] Following his break with Freud, Jung went through an extended period of strange dreams, trance states and waking visions, during which he encountered "personalities" in his psyche that he believed were not merely parts or aspects of himself, but were "objectively" real in their own right. It was out of this experience that Jung formulated his psychology. See "Confrontation with the Unconscious," in Jung's autobiography, *Memories, Dreams, Reflections* (London: Collins, 1967), pp. 194–225. See also my *Jung the Mystic* (New York: Tarcher/Penguin, 2010).

[27] See Ellenberger's classic work *The Discovery of the Unconscious* (London: Fontana, 1994).

[28] The most exhaustive account of hypnagogia remains Andreas Mavromatis's thorough study *Hypnagogia* (London: Routledge & Kegan Paul, 1987). Some of the people who have explored the hypnagogic state are Edgar Allan Poe, André Breton, Carl Jung, Jean-Paul Sartre, P. D. Ouspensky and the psychologist Julian Jaynes. For a brief account, see my article "Waking Sleep," in *Fortean Times*, no. 163, October 2002; http://www.forteantimes.com/features/articles/227/hypnagogia.html. See also my chapter "Hypnagogia," in *A Secret History of Consciousness.* In my essay "Swedenborg, Rudolf Steiner and the Hypnagogic State," in *The Arms of Morpheus—Essays on Swedenborg and Mysticism*, ed. Stephen McNeilly (London: Swedenborg Society, 2007), I examine the similarities between the visionary states of Swedenborg and Steiner, relating both to the hypnagogic state.

[29] Wilson Van Dusen, *The Presence of Other Worlds*, p. 25.

[30] Swedenborg, *The Spiritual Diary*, vol. I, §397.

[31] Robsahm's account of Swedenborg's story is almost certainly the inspiration for Jorge Louis Borges's dramatic embellishment that "A stranger

who had silently followed him [Swedenborg] through the streets of London, and about whose looks nothing is known, suddenly appeared in his room and told him he was the Lord." See Borges, "Testimony to the Invisible," in Swedenborg, *The Spiritual Diary*, vol. I, p. xxxix. Borges's essay is also published in other collections, Larsen (ed.), *Emanuel Swedenborg: A Continuing Vision*, and James F. Lawrence (ed.), *Testimony to the Invisible* (West Chester, PA: Chrysalis, 1995), an anthology of essays on Swedenborg, including contributions by Czeslaw Milosz, Kathleen Raine, D. T. Suzuki, Colin Wilson and others.

[32] Quoted in Wilson Van Dusen, *The Presence of Other Worlds*, p. 60. Toksvig (pp. 151–5) points out a discrepancy between Robsahm's account of this crucial encounter and the records Swedenborg himself made at or near the time: specifically that in both *The Spiritual Diary* and *The Word Explained*, in which Swedenborg again refers to the vapors emerging from his pores and of the worms and other like creatures appearing, there is no mention of the mysterious stranger, who is none other than the Lord, nor of the task which he is supposed to have given Swedenborg. Toksvig also points out that the other significant feature of the incident—that it was the start of Swedenborg's almost daily entrée into the spirit world—although mentioned several times in succeeding years, is not related to the event at the London inn. Swedenborg had been aware of "angelic voices" since his ecstatic states in 1743, and Toksvig points out that while writing his work on the brain, Swedenborg often felt that he had been "ordered" to write various things. Swedenborg's own terminology in the early part of his "mission" is vague and can lead to some confusion; he speaks of having felt the "sweetness and felicities" of the kingdom of God well in advance of his meeting with the mysterious stranger, although his descriptions of the "kingdom" then

lack the concreteness of his later spiritual travelogues. Toksvig's conclusion is that when Swedenborg related the experience to Robsahm, he unconsciously brought several different events together into a single, dramatic episode, providing his subsequent work with a heavenly imprimatur by invoking the Lord's presence. Swedenborg was aware of the possibility of error, and he knew that the mind can create a seemingly "objective" experience, which can nevertheless be traced back to some subjective, personal knowledge. The fact that the Lord asked Swedenborg if he had a "clean bill of health" is a case in point. Toksvig argues that Swedenborg wanted to believe in the truth of his experience, both because of the mission he had been given—to stop the slide into atheism—and also to keep his reason. Toksvig maintains, however, that it was not the reality of his encounter with Christ that convinced Swedenborg, but his meetings with those he knew who were dead. Christ's authority would raise Swedenborg's esoteric reading of the Bible above being merely his own interpretation, which would be one among many, to the status of "truth," but, so believes Toksvig, it was Swedenborg's unsought-for encounter with the dead that convinced him that his experiences were real.

[33] Wilson Van Dusen, *The Presence of Other Worlds*, p. 56.

[34] See Toksvig, pp. 246–7.

[35] Although seeing and hearing spirits is often considered evidence of madness, Wilson Van Dusen has suggested the opposite may be the case: that madness, specifically schizophrenia, may be a form of spirit-possession. See his chapter "The Presence of Spirits in Madness," in *The Presence of Other Worlds*.

[36] See Jaspers's *Strindberg und Van Gogh* (Munchen: R. Piper & Co. Verlag, 1949), which, along with Strindberg and Van Gogh, includes

Swedenborg and the German poet Hölderlin as case studies of schizophrenia. Although Steiner acknowledged that Swedenborg's visions were of "tremendous interest," they were, he thought, products of a "pathology." See Rudolf Steiner, *Fruits of Anthroposophy* (London: Rudolf Steiner Press, 1986), p. 28; also my essay "Swedenborg, Rudolf Steiner and the Hypnagogic State," mentioned above. Unfortunately, many spiritual and esoteric teachers have a tendency to "bad-mouth" each other. Steiner, who saw visions himself, was considered schizophrenic by C. G. Jung, and Jung, we know, had his own "psychotic" encounter. Steiner also had less than respectful words for Madame Blavatsky, the co-founder of Theosophy, and G. I. Gurdjieff thought practically everyone else was a "candidate for the lunatic asylum."

[37] T. S. Eliot, *The Complete Poems & Plays* (London: Faber and Faber, 2004), p. 89.

[38] Swedenborg, *The Spiritual Diary*, vol. I, §651.

[39] A comparison of Swedenborg's visions with those of an early explorer of lucid dreams, Frederik Van Eeden, strikes me as suggestive. Van Eeden charted several different types of dreams, one of which he called the "demon dream." In this type of dream, Van Eeden encountered entities similar to Swedenborg's "evil spirits." Van Eeden's fascinating essay "A Study of Dreams" can be found in Charles Tart's classic anthology *Altered States of Consciousness* (New York: Doubleday, 1972), pp. 147–60.

[40] Toksvig, p. 221.

[41] Friedrich Rittelmeyer, *Rudolf Steiner Enters My Life* (London: George Roberts, 1929), pp. 61–2.

Chapter Four

[1] Bergquist, p. 167.

[2] Swedenborg, *The Economy of the Animal Kingdom*, tr. Augustus Clissold (New York: New Church Press, 1919; repr. Swedenborg Scientific Association, 1955), vol. I, p. 464.

[3] Swedenborg, *The Worlds in Space*, tr. John Chadwick (London: Swedenborg Society, 1997), §158.3, p. 115.

[4] See Steiner's *Autobiography*, tr. Rita Stebbing (New York: Rudolf Steiner Publications, 1977), pp. 222–3. For Steiner's experiences with the dead, see pp. 251–8.

[5] Swedenborg, *Heaven and Hell*, tr. George F. Dole (New York: Swedenborg Foundation, 1984), §89, p. 81.

[6] Ibid.

[7] Ibid.

[8] Czeslaw Milosz, "Introduction" to *The Noble Traveller: The Life and Writings of O. V. de L Milosz*, p. 33.

[9] See my essay "The Spiritual Detective: How Baudelaire invented Symbolism, by way of Swedenborg, E. T. A. Hoffmann and Edgar Allan Poe," in Stephen McNeilly (ed.), *Between Method and Madness: Essays on Swedenborg and Literature* (London: Swedenborg Society, 2005), pp. 31–44. See also my *A Dark Muse: A History of the Occult* (New York: Thunder's Mouth Press, 2005).

[10] For more on Baudelaire's and Rimbaud's debt to the hermetic tradition, see my *A Dark Muse: A History of the Occult.*

[11] Anna Balakian, *The Symbolist Movement* (New York: New York University Press, 1977), p. 47.

[12] It is unclear how much Shaw had read of Swedenborg. He would have also arrived at such ideas from his reading of Blake.

[13] Bernard Shaw, *The Complete Plays of Bernard Shaw* (London: Odhams Press, Ltd., 1934), pp. 373–4.

[14] Swedenborg, *Heaven and Hell*, §403, pp. 312–13.

[15] Ibid., §421, p. 330.

[16] Ibid., §26, p. 42.

[17] Ibid., §457, p. 355.

[18] Shaw, *The Complete Plays of Bernard Shaw*, p. 374.

[19] Czeslaw Milosz, "Introduction," *The Noble Traveller: The Life and Writings of O. V. de L Milosz*, p. 34.

[20] Space doesn't allow me to do more than mention that Corbin's "cognitive imagination" has a respectable pedigree, including within it, among others, Goethe's "disciplined imagination," which later became the basis for Rudolf Steiner's "supersensible perception." It is also at the root of Jung's "active imagination," and is the "place" of such imaginative experiences as dreams and hypnagogic visions.

[21] Ralph Waldo Emerson, *Swedenborg: Introducing the Mystic*, ed. Stephen McNeilly (London: Swedenborg Society, 2009), pp. 10–11, 40.

[22] Swedenborg, *Heaven and Hell*, §586, pp. 489–90.

[23] Sir Oliver Lodge, *Raymond or Life and Death* (London: Metheun & Co., Ltd., 1916).

[24] Swedenborg, *Heaven and Hell*, §162, p. 129.

[25] Ibid., §191, p. 145.

[26] Ibid., §192, p. 145.

[27] Swedenborg, *The Worlds in Space*, §127, p. 93.

[28] For a look at how Swedenborg's ideas about space influenced another profound spiritual thinker, see my essay "Space: the Final Frontier: O. V. de Lubicz Milosz and Swedenborg," in Stephen McNeilly (ed.), *Between Method and Madness*.

[29] Robert Avens, "The Subtle Realm: Corbin, Sufism and Swedenborg," in Larsen (ed.), *Emanuel Swedenborg: A Continuing Vision*, pp. 387–8.

[30] Rainer Maria Rilke, *The Selected Poetry of Rainer Maria Rilke*, ed. and tr. Stephen Mitchell (New York: Vintage Books, 1984), p. 151.

[31] Ibid., p. 155.

[32] Walter Benjamin, *Illuminations*, ed. Hannah Arendt, tr. Harry Zohn (London: Fontana Press, 1992), p. 249.

[33] Swedenborg, *Heaven and Hell*, §240, p. 173.

[34] Ibid., §261, p. 188.

[35] Ibid., §239, p. 172.

[36] Ibid., §239.2, pp. 172–3.

[37] For more on angelic speech and numbers, see the chapters "Angels' Language," "Angels' Speech with Man," and "Written Materials in Heaven," in *Heaven and Hell*, §§234–64, pp. 170–90.

[38] William James, "On Some Hegelianisms," in *Mindscapes: An Anthology of Drug Writings*, ed. Antonio Melechi (West Yorkshire: Mono Press, 1998), pp. 20–2.

[39] P. D. Ouspensky, *A New Model of the Universe* (New York: Alfred A. Knopf, 1969), pp. 277–8.

[40] Ibid., pp. 280–1.

[41] Ibid., p. 288.

[42] Ibid., pp. 289–90.

[43] Ibid., p. 279.

Select Bibliography of Swedenborg's Works

Daedalus Hyperboreus (pub. 1716–18)

At the age of twenty-six, after having spent several years in London and Paris studying Newton, Halley, Malebranche, Leibniz et al., Swedenborg returned to Sweden keen to put his learning to some use. He got the opportunity with *Daedalus Hyperboreus*, Sweden's first scientific journal. Following the template of the *Philosophical Transactions* of the Royal Society in Britain, it was written in Swedish with the aim of popularizing the practical sciences and mathematics. Swedenborg edited and financed the journal, drawing up and publishing the mechanical inventions of Christopher Polhem and others, but also featuring his own designs for a flying machine, ear trumpet, hoisting machinery and air pump. In the fourth issue, he published his method for determining longitude at sea, a project that would preoccupy him for the next forty years. Swedenborg presented a bound edition of the first four numbers to King Charles XII. Charles was impressed, and Swedenborg was subsequently awarded a position on the Board of Mines. There is currently no complete English translation.

The Principia (pub. 1734)

Between 1718 and 1734, Swedenborg worked on numerous manuscripts and articles on mineralogy and politics, but the *Opera Philosophica et Mineralia* marked his first mature work of philosophy. The opening volume—entitled *The Principia; or, the First Principles of Natural Things*, in the manner of Newton's *Principia*—marked his ambitious attempt at establishing a system for understanding the origins and mechanics of the universe (from the simplest and least particle or point up to "the ultimate compound," to our earth and the universe). Completed by Swedenborg at the age of fourty-six, he reasons that the creation of the finite is from the infinite, describing the necessity and nature (vortical) of motion and of magnetism. In building up from the least, Swedenborg comes to the origin of our solar system, and his cosmology contains a forerunner of the nebular hypothesis usually attributed to Kant and Laplace. Volumes two and three dealt with mining and the processing of copper and iron. Current English edition: *The Principia*, tr. Rev. Augustus Clissold, 2 vols. (Bryn Athyn, PA: Swedenborg Scientific Association, 1988).

The Infinite. The Final Cause of Creation (pub. 1734)

During the printing of *The Principia*, Swedenborg continued his investigations into the origins of the finite in the infinite by writing and printing *The Infinite*. Divided into two parts, the first part sees Swedenborg place his arguments in the context of rational metaphysics, stating that man is the final cause of Creation as he is able to acknowledge the infinite (i.e., God); and that the nexus between the finite and infinite is Christ. The second part, written in response to Descartes, Wolff and Leibniz, tackles the interaction between the soul and the body, a subject that Swedenborg would return to repeatedly. Current English edition: *The Infinite. The Final Cause of Creation*, tr. J. J. G. Wilkinson (London: Swedenborg Society, 1992).

The Economy of the Animal Kingdom (pub. 1740–1)

In the seven years since the publication of *The Principia*, Swedenborg had shifted his attention from a study of the universe and natural world to a study of the soul. Citing from anatomical sources such as Leeuwenhoek, Boerhaave, Harvey, Malpighi and many others, the first part of *The Economy of the Animal Kingdom* focuses on blood (the "epitome of the riches of the whole world and all its kingdoms . . . all things were created for the purpose of administering to . . . the blood") and its circulation. Swedenborg sees the soul as present everywhere in the body descending in degrees through the "spirituous fluid" and the "purer blood," both contained within the red blood, which is charged with carrying out the soul's functions in the body. The second part is on the brain. R. W. Emerson was especially impressed by the work, describing it as "one of those books which by the sustained dignity of thinking is an honour to the human race." Current English edition: *Dynamics of the Soul's Domain*, tr. Rev. Augustus Clissold, 2 vols. (Bryn Athyn, PA: Swedenborg Scientific Association, 2009).

The Cerebrum (1738–40) and The Brain (1742–3)

During his work on the soul, Swedenborg also drafted several works on the brain, conceived, varyingly, as parts of his *The Economy of the Animal Kingdom* and the later *The Animal Kingdom* series; yet aside from using a fraction of reworked material in the second volume of *The Economy,* in each case these works were left unpublished in manuscript form. As early as 1734, in *The Infinite*, Swedenborg had placed the soul in the cortical and medullary parts of the cerebrum, and he promised to demonstrate this physiologically in a later work. *The Cerebrum* appears to be that promised work, but for some reason Swedenborg chose not to publish, switching from a study of the brain to that of the blood instead. Swedenborg's discoveries were long in advance of their time, greatly impressing the scientific world with their anticipation on eventual publication at the end of the nineteenth century. Current English editions: *The Cerebrum*, tr. A. Acton, 2 vols. (Bryn Athyn, PA: Swedenborg Scientific Association, 2005); *The Brain Considered Anatomically, Physiologically, and Philosophically*, tr. R. L. Tafel, 2 vols. (Bryn Athyn, PA: Swedenborg Scientific Association, 2005).

A Philosopher's Notebook (1741–4)

In addition to his anatomical and scientific studies, and during the period in which he was compiling *The Economy* and *The Cerebrum*, Swedenborg kept a series of notebooks and journals for private use. The *Philosopher's Notebook* is one such journal and is of particular interest because it contains extracts copied from various philosophers, theologians, mathematicians and the Bible, revealing his influences. The excerpts were to be used as references in his physiological works, and several drafts of outlines for his *The Economy of the Animal Kingdom* and *The Animal Kingdom* series are contained within. Swedenborg's sources range from the classical (Plato, Aristotle) via the Cartesian (Descartes, Malebranche) to his contemporaries (Wolff, Leibniz). The quotations are grouped under topic headings, many of which foreshadow his concerns as a theological writer. Swedenborg writes little of his own in the notebook, but his selections go a long way to revealing a unity between Swedenborg the scientist and

Swedenborg the seer-theosopher. Current English edition: *A Philosopher's Notebook*, tr. Alfred Acton (Bryn Athyn, PA: Swedenborg Scientific Association, 2009).

The Animal Kingdom (pub. 1744–5)

The second and last of Swedenborg's great physiological works. It follows in the same vein as *The Economy of the Animal Kingdom*, with copious citations from leading anatomical authorities and conclusions from the evidence gathered. *The Animal Kingdom* was to be the start of a work planned to cover the entire anatomical structure. It covers the digestive and respiratory systems, the liver, pancreas, spleen, kidneys and the start of an inquiry into the senses, looking at touch and taste. Swedenborg gave up his project in 1745, after his spiritual illumination, leaving the remainder of his planned work in unpublished manuscripts. Current English edition: *The Soul's Domain*, tr. J. J. G. Wilkinson, 2 vols. (Bryn Athyn, PA: Swedenborg Scientific Association, 2009).

Journal of Dreams (1743–4)

This small pocket book, which lay hidden in the library of a professor in the Swedish town of Västerås until 1858, was Swedenborg's journal for the years 1743–4 and marks, after his sojourns in science and philosophy, the third and final turning point of Swedenborg's career. The first entries resemble those of his previous travel journals, but the bulk of the text is a record of Swedenborg's dreams from March to October of 1744, a period when Swedenborg was in Holland and London to publish the first volumes of his work on anatomy and the seat of the soul in the human body, *The Animal Kingdom*. The dreams and spiritual experiences recorded reflect the crisis Swedenborg was undergoing. He had become disillusioned with his scientific and philosophical work and was disgusted by his yearning for recognition and fame. The entries in the diary vacillate from despair to contentment as Swedenborg searches for the path to follow. Of major significance is that Swedenborg did not just log the details of his dreams, but also provided his own analysis of their meaning—at times in context of the anatomical writing he was concurrently engaged with, at others in relation to the spiritual epiphanies he was having. *The Journal of Dreams* is therefore one of the earliest dream analyses and it has attracted the attention of psychoanalysts, professional and amateur, ever since its discovery. Current English edition: *Swedenborg's Dream Diary*, with commentary by Lars Bergquist, tr. Anders Hallengren (West Chester, PA: Swedenborg Foundation, 2001).

The Worship and Love of God (pub. 1745)

During and following his spiritual crisis, Swedenborg began writing *The Worship and Love of God*. This curious work, full of classical allusions, showing the influence of Ovid and written in a florid style, tells the story of the first chapters of Genesis: the Creation, and the first days of Adam and Eve. In subject matter the book points toward the biblical exegesis he would soon undertake; in style it hearkens back to his first literary pursuits as a poet; and in the lengthy footnotes that run throughout the text is contained the knowledge Swedenborg gleaned from his scientific, philosophical and anatomical studies. One footnote alone, in which he described the formation of the firmament (the stars beyond our solar system), particularly impressed S. T. Coleridge, who commented: "Note (b) would of itself suffice to mark Swedenborg as a man of philosophic genius, radicative and evol-vent." Current English edition: *The Worship and Love of God*, tr. Alfred Stroh and Frank Sewall (London: Swedenborg Society, 1996).

The Word Explained (1745–7)

Soon after abandoning the final section of *The Worship and Love of God,* Swedenborg began a study of the Bible, and produced four large folio volumes containing more than 2,000 manuscript pages of detailed biblical commentary. *The Word Explained*, as the work has been posthumously entitled, offers an analysis of the "Historical Word" of the Old Testament (Genesis through to 2 Chronicles) and a start on the "Prophetical Word" with an examination of Isaiah and Jeremiah. Swedenborg learned Hebrew for the project, and we see him feeling his way to a description of the internal sense of the Word and the Doctrine of Correspondences. Importantly, *The Word Explained* also contains the first descriptions by Swedenborg of his spiritual and visionary experiences (making up the earliest entries of *The Spiritual Diary*), and these are interspersed among the scriptural explications. Current English edition: *The Word Explained*, tr. Alfred Acton, 9 vols. (Bryn Athyn, PA: Academy of the New Church, 1929–51).

The Spiritual Diary (1745–65)

The sporadic descriptions of his spiritual experiences in *The Word Explained* form part of a documentation that would continue for the next twenty years. The record of these accounts is *The Spiritual Diary*. Swedenborg would often rework entries as memorabilia in his published works, but though unpolished, the material in *The Spiritual Diary* is often more interesting, as we are presented with the image of a man trying to describe and map the entire structure of a world not seen before. *The Spiritual*

Diary is less guarded than his other accounts, and we see descriptions of the fates of many famous people in the next life, as well as of Swedenborg's personal and professional acquaintances. Striving for analogies between spiritism, folklore, religion and Neoplatonism, the poet W. B. Yeats "opened *The Spiritual Diary* . . . and found all there." Current English edition: *The Spiritual Diary*, ed. Stephen McNeilly (vol. I, tr. A. W. Acton; vols. II–III, tr. G. Bush and J. H. Smithson; vol. IV, tr. G. Bush and J. F. Buss; vol. V, tr. J. F. Buss), 5 vols. (London: Swedenborg Society, 2002–).

Arcana Coelistia (pub. 1749–56)

Arcana Coelistia is a study of the first two books of the Bible—Genesis and Exodus—in light of Swedenborg's task of revealing the internal or spiritual, as opposed to literal, sense of the Word. *Arcana Coelistia* is his key theosophical work, with most of his later works in one way or another reflecting upon it. In the course of a verse-by-verse account, Swedenborg describes the contents of his theology: the Grand Man, the Doctrine of Correspondences, the nature of the Trinity, the succeeding ages of the Churches, the dualities of love/wisdom, good/truth, faith/charity and much more. In between the chapters of biblical exegesis, he inserted memorabilia—accounts of what he had heard and seen in the spiritual world, in heaven, and in hell. Current English edition: *Arcana Coelistia*, tr. John Elliott, 12 vols. (London: Swedenborg Society, 1983–99).

The Worlds in Space (pub. 1758)

Along with the other titles published in 1758, this work consists of reworked extracts from *Arcana Coelistia*. It has since become the most controversial of Swedenborg's books. Swedenborg says that there is life elsewhere in the universe, even within our solar system, and that this life is intelligent and human too. He meets the spirits of the dead of these planets, learning how they lived and what they believe. There are belching Lunarians, data-collecting Mercurians, and horse-fearing Jovians. His encounters lead him to reflect on how we humans on earth live, and how in successive ages we have moved further and further away from the spiritual to the corporeal side of things. The book (we are the only planet that uses the written word, incidentally) still serves as an excellent introduction to Swedenborg, as he often uses his adventures as a launching point to explain simply and concisely the workings of the world of spirits, heaven and hell, and the theology he has derived from his otherworldly travels. Current English edition: *The Worlds in Space*, tr. Dr. John Chadwick (London: Swedenborg Society, 1996; repr. as *Life on Other Planets* with foreword by Dr. Raymond Moody, 2006).

Heaven and Hell (pub. 1758)

Swedenborg's most famous work, and one that has now been translated into over thirty languages. Swedenborg gives an explorer's account of his voyages in heaven, hell and the intermediary world of spirits, and explains the processes we undergo after death. Swedenborg's afterlife in many ways resembles our earthly life: our spirits have bodies and senses, wear clothes, have duties and homes. In its precision and detail, *Heaven and Hell* was a marked departure from the teachings of the then existing Christian Churches on life after death, and as such it has attracted many readers over the last two hundred and fifty years and its influence on our perceptions today can scarcely be measured. Current English edition: *Heaven and Hell*, tr. K. C. Ryder (London: Swedenborg Society, 2010).

The New Jerusalem and Its Heavenly Doctrine (pub. 1758)

This small book is Swedenborg's attempt to outline his key theological points in short, digestible chapters. Mankind, for Swedenborg, had gone through four ages which could be distinguished into churches: the Most Ancient Church (antediluvian), the Ancient Church (Noachian), the Israelite Church (the Jewish Church of the Old Testament) and the Christian Church. As Swedenborg was writing, the Christian Church was drawing to an end, and Catholicism had moved away from God, denying people the chance to read the Word of God and elevating Papal authority to an equal or superior standing to that of Scripture. Meanwhile, the Reformed Churches were putting too much emphasis on matters of faith at the expense of love and charity. In 1757 a last judgment took place in heaven and the spiritual world, Swedenborg tells us, clearing the way for a new age. In *The New Jerusalem*, Swedenborg summarizes the teachings of this age, discussing the meaning and importance of "good" and "truth," describing human nature and how to live a good life through love of God and charity. Current English edition: *Introducing the New Jerusalem*, tr. John Chadwick, ed. Stephen McNeilly (London: Swedenborg Society, 2006).

Conjugial Love (pub. 1768)

Swedenborg published his work on sex, love and marriage as an eighty-year-old bachelor. It was the first of his theological works not to be published anonymously. In *Conjugial Love*, Swedenborg describes true marriage love as the greatest heavenly delight, being a marriage of good and truth. True marriage love is little known today, Swedenborg informs us, but those united by it will continue to be so after death, married partners conjoining to such an extent that they appear as one angel. Swedenborg described *Conjugial*

Love as "a book of morals," and within it he stresses the equality of married partners, departing from the commonly held views and practices of the time of male dominance and female subordination. Current English edition: *Conjugial Love*, tr. John Chadwick (London: Swedenborg Society, 1996).

The True Christian Religion (pub. 1771)

The last book to be published by Swedenborg, *The True Christian Religion* is his theological *summa*, and his treatment of the main tenets of theology: the Trinity, the Bible, the Ten Commandments, faith, charity, free will, repentance, baptism and the Eucharist. The work seems to be addressed to a primarily Lutheran audience, for it was, in part, written as a refutation of the accusation of heresy leveled at Swedenborg's writings by the Gothenburg Consistory in 1769. (At this time Sweden was a Lutheran country with strict censorship legislation, which was why Swedenborg published his works in Britain and Holland. However, two of his followers had published Bible expositions based on his teachings in Sweden, and were subsequently put on trial.) Swedenborg wanted to use approved Lutheran authorities to demonstrate that his teaching was not only not heretical, but was in fact "True Christianity." In *The True Christian Religion*, Swedenborg was presenting not just a summary of his theology, but a proposal to rethink and recast the traditional doctrine of Lutheranism and all Christian Churches. Current English edition: *The True Christian Religion*, tr. Dr. John Chadwick, 2 vols. (London: Swedenborg Society, 1988).

Index

Absolute, the, 46
Adam, 84, 89
afterlife, the, 115, 122; *see also* heaven; hell; spirit world, the
Akashic Record, the, xvii, 96, 97
alchemy, xiv, xxii, 2, 15, 112; alchemical formula, 17, 46; alchemical laboratory, 23; alchemists, 22, 24
alienation, 79
Amsterdam, 14, 20, 23, 82
anatomy, 26, 52, 53, 59; *see also* blood; brain, the
ancients, the, 111
angels, xv, 7, 8, 9, 12, 21, 22, 31, 46, 50, 55, 84, 86, 88, 89, 91, 94, 98, 103–4, 106, 115, 116, 117, 119, 122–9, 134, 135; celestial, 127; Gabriel, 123; language of, 124, 127–9, 134
anima, 52, 65, 66; *see also* soul
animals, 52, 63, 66
anthropic cosmological principle, the, 49
Apostles, the, 92
appetites, 63, 66, 67, 74, 116, 120; *see also* desires
Aristotle, 16
Arrhenius, Svante, 48
"as above, so below," 17, 46, 112
astonishing hypothesis, the, 39, 60
astral body, 62, 63, 65
astral traveling, 98
astrology, xiv
astronomy, 16, 24, 25, 37, 48
atoms, 44–5, 60, 62
auras, 12, 64, 65
automata, 28
automatic writing, 23
Avens, Robert, 125, 126, 135

Ba'al Shem, 23
Balakian, Anna, 114
Balsamo, Giuseppe, *see* Cagliostro

Balzac, Honoré de, xvii, 123; *Seraphita*, 123
Barrow, John, 49
Baudelaire, Charles, xvii, 113, 114; "Correspondances," xvii, 113
Beckford, William, 71
Beethoven, Ludwig van, 28, 110
Behaviorism, 60
Behm, Sara, 4, 6, 7, 9
Benjamin, Walter, 126; angel of history, 126
Benzelius, Erik, 14–16, 18, 19, 24, 26, 29
Bergia, Sara, 6, 7, 33
Bergquist, Lars, 4, 103
Bergson, Henri, 57
Bible, xviii, xix, xx, xxii, xxiii, 16, 24, 26, 57, 84, 85, 101, 111, 113; Exodus, xix, 102; Genesis, xix, 102; Gospels, 4; Old Testament, 15; Revelation, 102; *see also* Scripture
bipolar syndrome, 12
Blake, Catherine, 21
Blake, James, 21
Blake, William, 8, 21, 28, 79, 119, 121; *The Marriage of Heaven and Hell*, 119
blood, 10, 54, 103
Board of Trade, the, 107
Bodleian Library, 25
body and its relationship with soul, 9, 40, 52–6, 62, 64–7; *see also* soul; Swedenborg, search for soul
Boehme, Jacob, 24, 51
Boerhaave, Herman, 52
Bohm, David, 42, 43; the explicate order, 42; the implicate order, 42, 43
Bosch, Hieronymus, 120
brain, the, xx, 9, 10, 12, 40, 43, 52–5, 61, 78, 79, 80, 97; cerebellum, 55, 56; cerebral cortex, 53; cerebrospinal fluid, 54; frontal lobes, 55; ganglia, 54; gray matter, 53, 54; hippocampus, 97; limbic system, 12, 97; medulla oblongata, 97; motion of, 9, 54; neocortex, 97; optic lobes, 54; pineal gland, 52; pituitary gland, 54; pre-cortical structures, 97; "reptilian brain," 12; spinal cord, 54; thalamus, 97; "triune brain," 12
breath, control of, 9–11, 13, 23, 40, 77–8; *see also* meditation; respiration
Bremen, 73
Brunsbo, 14, 19
Buddhism, Tibetan, xix
Burroughs, William S., 120
Butler, Samuel, 57

Cagliostro, xxii, 22
Cambridge Platonists, the, 59
canon, esoteric, 17; Western 101
carbon dioxide, 10
Catholicism, 117
cerebellum, *see* brain, the
cerebrum, *see* brain, the
chain of being, 46, 63
chance, 88; and cosmology 50, 56–8
chaos theory, 44

Charles XII, 19, 29, 31, 32, 37
chivalry, 90
Christ, 50, 51, 78, 85, 86, 92; *see also* Lord, the
Christianity, xvi, 10, 22, 51, 101; *see also* Church
Church, 8, 61, 119; Eastern Orthodox, 10; New, 21
clairvoyance, xvi, xviii, 108; *see also* precognition; telepathy
classics, 16; *see also* Greek; Latin
Clerkenwell, 7
Coleridge, Samuel Taylor, 30
conjugial, love, 31, 90, 112; union, 89
consciousness, 9, 10, 12, 13, 39, 53, 54, 55, 56, 59, 60, 61, 72, 78, 80, 87, 88, 94, 98, 104, 115, 117, 119, 129, 130, 131, 133, 134; *see also* experience; subjective
Corbin, Henry, 119
correspondences, 18, 55, 64, 111–14; *see also* signs; symbols
cosmology, xx, 46, 49
cosmos, the, 28, 32, 46, 48, 49, 50, 79; *see also* space; universe, the
Creation, 17, 46, 47, 84, 89, 126
Creationism, 57
Crick, Francis, 38, 39, 60; the astonishing hypothesis, 39, 60
culture, 12, 105; popular, xiii; post-, xix; Western, xvii, 79

daimon, 41
Dante Alighieri, 120, 124; *Inferno*, 120
Darwin, Charles, 57; evolution, 57, 58; natural selection, 57; Darwinian, 57, 58, 59
Dasein, 128
da Vinci, Leonardo, xx, 26
Da Vinci Code, *The*, xxii
dead, the, 91, 108, 109, 110, 117, 118, 125, 126; *see also* spirit(s)
Degrees, *see* Doctrine of Series and Degrees
Denmark, 19, 20, 73
Dennett, Daniel, 39; *Consciousness Explained*, 39
depression, 12, 84
De Quincey, Thomas, 24
Descartes, René, 15, 16, 39, 52; free inquiry, 16; mechanical philosophy of, 15
desires, 62, 63, 65, 66, 67, 72, 75, 81, 117, 120; *see also* appetites
despair, 82, 84
Devil, the, 116; devils, 119
dimensionless points, 42, 44, 47, 48, 51, 65; *see also* elementary particles
Divine, the, 6, 15, 17, 23, 45, 51, 55, 56, 59, 112, 124; divine grace, 104; divine territories, 115; divine truth and love, 112, 124; divine understanding, 124; *see also* God; Lord, the
DNA, 39, 58
Doctrine of Series and Degrees, 61, 62, 63, 64, 65, 124
Don Juan, 115, 116
Donna Ana, 116

"double thoughts," 82, 85, 92, 93; *see also* Swedenborg, spiritual crisis and doubt of
dreams, 2, 71, 72, 73, 74, 75, 76, 77, 78, 79, 81, 87, 97, 98, 116, 129; lucid, 95, 98; precognitive, 82, 105; sexual, 74–7
Driesch, Hans, 57
Drury Lane, 28
Dürrenmatt, Friedrich, 126; *An Angel Comes to Babylon*, 126

earth, the, 23, 47, 48, 49, 59, 86, 115, 117, 118, 122, 123, 126, 128; earthly, 3, 6, 7, 17, 23, 30, 51, 115, 122
East End, the, 21, 23
Edison, Thomas, 26
ego, the, 3, 62, 63, 67, 72, 73, 87
eidetic imagery, 95
Einstein, Albert, xvii
electricity, 64
elementary particles, 42, 44; elements, 42, 44, 111; *see also* dimensionless points
Eliot, T. S., 93; "Ash Wednesday," 93
Ellenberger, Henri, 87
emanationism, 17, 45
embryo, 56
Emerson, Ralph Waldo, xvi, 81, 119, 120
emotions, 12, 62, 79, 80, 130; hellish, 121; religious, 89
enantiodromia, 2
Encyclopaedia Britannica, 95
energy, 44, 45, 52
engineering, xx, 32
England, 18, 19, 21, 24, 47, 59, 106
Enlightenment, the, xiv, xv, 114
entopic forms, 41
epilepsy, 12, 13, 41
epistemology, xviii
erotic, eroticism, 22, 23, 31, 51, 55, 74, 76, 77, 89, 121; *see also* sex
esoteric, esotericism, xv, xvi, xvii, xviii, xix, xx, xxii, 3, 15, 17, 21, 22, 23, 24, 46, 51, 62, 66, 95, 101, 105, 109
ESP, 14
eternity, 52, 115, 117, 123
ether, the, 64; etheric body, 62; etheric forces, 58, 62
Eve, 84, 89
evil, 82, 83; spirits, 11, 86, 91, 94
evolution, 57, 58
existentialism, 51, 79, 92
Exodus, xix, 102
experience, xix, 10, 25, 31, 51, 56, 67, 71, 73, 79, 80, 85, 87, 90, 105, 109, 113, 121, 129, 130, 131; author's personal, xiv; inner/interior, 1, 40, 60, 79, 87; mystical/paranormal, 55, 65, 105, 128, 129, 130, 134; out-of-body, 85, 98; "peak," 55; religious, 81; Swedenborg's spiritual, xx, 1, 3, 6, 11, 12, 40, 49, 65, 78, 79, 85, 86, 92, 101, 104, 134; *see also* consciousness; subjective
explicate order, the, 42

Falk, Rabbi Samuel Jacob Hayyim, 22, 23

fear, 63, 77, 132
fibers, 54
finite, the, 38, 41, 50, 51, 78
Flamsteed, John, 24
Fodor's guide, 73
formative substance, 56, 57, 58, 62
fractals, 44, 45, 46
Fredrikshald, 32
Freemasons, xxii, 22
Freud, Sigmund, 72, 74; Freudian, 86

Gabriel, the angel, 123
Galicia, 23
Garrick, David, 28
Genesis, xix, 102
geology, 37; *see also* mineralogy
geometry, 41, 42
Gilchrist, Alexander, 21; *Life of William Blake*, 21
Gnosis, xvi
God, xvi, 3, 5, 8, 9, 12, 17, 38, 39, 51, 57, 80, 83, 84, 88, 107, 123; *see also* Divine, the; Lord, the
Goethe, Johann Wolfgang von, xvii, 57, 58, 79, 112
Gooch, Stan, 55, 56
Gospels, 4
Gothenburg, 106, 107
grace, 5, 12, 60, 83, 85, 92, 104
Grand Man, the, 46, 104, 124
Grand Tour, the, 20
Greek, 2, 16, 72
Greenwich Observatory, 25
Groningen, 73
Gurdjieff, G. I., 46, 47, 95; Absolute, the, 46; Ray of Creation, 46, 47
Gyllenborg, Countess Elizabeth Stierncrona, 30, 31, 33
Gyllenborg, Count Frederic, 30, 33

Halley, Edmund, 25
Hamburg, 20, 23, 25
Hanoverians, the, xxii
Harlingen, 73
Harrison, John, 25
heart, the, xviii, 54, 55
heat, 64
heaven, xv, xviii, 6, 7, 11, 12, 23, 27, 30, 31, 46, 50, 51, 55, 59, 67, 89, 90, 91, 92, 94, 95, 96, 98, 101, 102, 103, 104, 111, 114, 115, 116, 117, 118, 119, 121, 122, 123, 124, 125, 126, 127, 128, 133, 134; activity in, 117; geography or cartography of, 55, 67, 94, 101
Hebraist, 15
Hebrew, 15, 72
Heidegger, Martin, 128; *Dasein*, 128
hell, xviii, 2, 12, 14, 76, 85, 89, 91, 96, 98, 101, 102, 104, 114, 115, 116, 117, 118, 119, 120, 121, 133
Heller, Erich, 77
Helsingborg, 20
heresy, 23, 59, 91
Hermes Trismegistus, 113, 128
hermetic, thought/thinkers, 17, 24, 46; tradition, 15, 17, 112
Hermetic Order of the Golden Dawn, the, 22
Herrnhuters, *see* Moravian Brethren, the

hippocampus, *see* brain, the
history, xiv, xix, xxiv; angel of, 126; of consciousness, xxiii; of esoteric/occult, xv, 21, 98, 103, 105; of ideas, xiii; as a subject of study, 16
Holland, 23, 25
Hollywood, 90
hologram, 43–6, 135
holons, 47
House of Nobles, 33; *see also* Parliament
humanism, Renaissance, 15
Humphrey, Nicholas, 38, 39
Huxley, Aldous, xxi, 10; *Doors of Perception*, 10; *Heaven and Hell*, 10
hypnagogia, 87, 94, 97, 98, 104
hypocrisy, 6, 18, 22, 31, 118

illusion(s), illusory, 38, 42, 59, 60
imagination, 29, 96, 98, 110, 119
immaterial, 38, 58, 59, 61
implicate order, the, 42, 43
individuation, 72–3
infinite, infinity, 32, 38, 42, 44, 45, 46, 47, 50, 51, 52, 65, 78, 114, 115, 124, 125, 130, 132, 134, 135
infinitesimal points, 45
Inquisition, the, xxii
interior or inner world, xviii, xxi, 40, 60, 61, 62, 77, 78, 79, 81, 87, 95, 96, 112
Internet, 90
Italy, 52

Jacobson, Ludwig Levin, 13
Jacobson's organ, 13, 14
James, Henry Sr., 82
James, William, 82, 83, 128, 129, 130, 131, 133, 134, 135; "A Suggestion about Mysticism," 128; *The Varieties of Religious Experience*, 82
Jaspers, Karl, 92
Jehovah's Witnesses, xvi
Jewish, xix, 15, 23, 126
journey within, 77, 80, 93, 95, 135
Jung, Carl Gustav, xvi, 2, 65, 72, 77, 86, 98; Jungians, 75; *enantiodromia*, 2; individuation, 72–3
Jupiter, 49

Kabbala Denudata, 15
Kabbalah, xix, 15, 22, 23, 24, 31, 51, 127; Kabbalists, xxii, 22, 24, 128
Kammerer, Paul, 57
Kant, Immanuel, xvii, xviii, 48, 106; *Critique of Pure Reason*, xviii; *Dreams of a Spirit Seer*, xvii; *noumena*, xviii; *phenomena*, xviii
Karlskrona, 31
Kempelen, Wolfgang von, 28
Kierkegaard, Søren, 51
Klee, Paul, 126; *Angelus Novus*, 126
Knights Templar, xxii
Knorr von Rosenroth, Christian, 15; *Kabbala Denudata*, 15
Koestler, Arthur, 47, 57

Lamarck, Jean Baptiste, 57

Laplace, Pierre Simon de, 48
Larsen, Stephen, 73
Latin, xviii, 16, 18, 40, 52, 74
law(s), xx, 16, 39, 47, 57, 58, 59, 60, 61, 62, 65; natural law, 16
Leer, 73
Leeuwarden, 73
Leeuwenhoek, Anton van, 52
Leibniz, Gottfried Wilhelm von, 15
light, 2, 40, 41, 43, 64, 65, 88, 96, 111, 112; as a "confirmatory" sign for Swedenborg, 40, 65, 78, 82; inner, 82
likepartedness, 45, 46
limbic system, the, 12, 97
limbo, 129
liver, the, 103
Lodge, Sir Oliver, 122; *Raymond or Life And Death*, 122
London, xx, xxi, 7, 14, 20, 21, 22, 23, 24, 25, 47, 86, 87, 91, 108; Clerkenwell, 7; Drury Lane, 28; the East End, 21, 23; Greenwich, 25; London Bridge, 23
longitude, 25, 29
Lord, the, 3, 5, 6, 81, 82, 86, 88, 89, 124; *see also* Christ; Divine, the; God
Louis XV, xxii
Louisa Ulrica, Queen of Sweden, 106, 107, 108, 109
Loutherbourg, Philip James de, 21, 22, 28
love, 7, 16, 30, 51, 52, 60, 62, 75, 80, 90, 103, 115, 118; conjugial, 31, 90, 112; divine, 112, 124; ruling, 32; self-, 5, 6, 26, 67, 79, 81, 116, 118; sexual, 30, 51, 66
LSD, 10
lungs, the, 9, 10, 54
Lutherans, theology of, 17

MacLean, Paul, 12
macrocosm, 46
magic, 112, 128; magician, xxii, 23
magnetism, 64
Malpighi, Marcello, 52
Mandelbrot, Benoit, 44
Mars, 49
Maslow, Abraham, 55
material, 41, 49, 58, 62, 65, 66, 84, 125, 132; body, 59; genetic, 58; stellar, 49; world, 114; materialist, xiv, 39, 62; matter, 44, 57, 58, 59, 60, 62, 63; inorganic, 57, 58; organic, 53, 58
mathematics, 16, 24, 31; mathematical, 44, 45; mathematician, 44, 48
Mathesius, Pastor Aaron, 91
Mavromatis, Andreas, 97; *Hypnagogia*, 97
McLuhan, Marshall, 64
medicine, 16
meditation, 40, 41; *see also* breath, control of
mediums, 122
melancholy, 82, 83, 84
memory, 39, 43, 61
mens, 66
mescaline, 10
Messiah complex, 92

metaphysics, xviii, xx, 17, 23; metaphysical, 32, 38, 130
microcosm, 46, 63
Milan, 20
Milky Way, the, 48, 49
Milosz, Czeslaw, 112, 119
mineralogy, mining, xx, xxi, 33, 37, 38; of copper, 38, 124; of iron, 38; saltworks, 32; Swedish Board of Mines, 4, 21, 31, 32, 82, 92, 93
miracles, 56, 84
molecules, 39, 58, 60, 62
Monod, Jacques, 56; *Chance and Necessity*, 56
moon, the, 46, 47, 49; lunar, 29
Moravian Brethren, the, 22, 91
morphic resonance, 57
morphogenetic fields, 58
Moses, 84
mouth, the, 11, 85
Mozart, Wolfgang Amadeus, 95
mystical, xix, 17, 51, 56, 134; experiences/states, 10, 55, 65, 128, 130, 133, 134; thinkers, 85; tradition, 15; mysticism, xiii, 18, 31, 128, 131; mystics, 13, 123

Napoleon I, 28
nature, xvii, 39, 57, 58, 59, 61, 113; human, 62, 66, 105; natural, 57, 67, 75, 111; heaven, 124; law, 16; thought, 127, 129; world, 111, 114
nebular hypothesis, the, 48
Neoplatonic, 45, 59, 65, 89; Neoplatonists, 17; *see also* Cambridge Platonists, the
nerves, 13, 39, 54, 103; intercostal, 103; par vagum, 103
neurons, 55, 61, 63
neurophysiology, 43; neuroscience, 38, 53, 59, 80; neurotransmitter, 52
New Age, 79–80
Newton, Sir Isaac, xxii, xxiii, 15, 24, 25, 39; Newtonian, 39, 42
nexus, 50, 51, 78
Nietzsche, Friedrich, 57, 110
nitrous oxide, 130, 131, 134
Nobel Prize, 48
North Sea, the, 19, 32
noumena, xviii
novae, *see* stars

Occam's Razor, 60
occult, xiii, xiv, xv, xvi, xix, xxii, xxiii, 98, 103, 105
odors, *see* smell
Old Testament, 15
Oldenburg, 73
oratory, 16
origins of life, 57, 58
Ouspensky, P. D., 46, 51, 130, 131, 132, 133, 134, 135; *A New Model of the Universe*, 131; *In Search of the Miraculous*, 46; *Tertium Organum*, 51
Oxford, 25
oxygen, 10

Palacios, Wilson, 176
Paradise, 89, 126
paralysis, 93

paranormal, xvi, 4, 14, 55, 56, 103, 104, 105, 122; *see also* supernatural
Paris, xx, 20, 25, 52
Parliament, Swedish, xx, 32, 37, 92; English, 30; *see also* House of Nobles
particle physics, 44
Percy, Walker, 79
phenomena, xiv, 2, 39, 51, 59, 60, 61, 62, 80, 82, 95, 105, 113, 133; Kantian, xviii
phenomenology, 94
pheromones, 13
Philo Judaeus, 15
photograph, 43–4; photographic detail, 95
physics, 44, 57; physicist, 42, 57
physical, body/shell, 60, 61, 62, 110; existence, 96; laws, 58, 62; phenomena, 59, 60; place/location, 119, 123; reality, 59; world, 38, 44, 45, 66, 111, 114
physiology, 52, 53; physiological, 9
pietists, 22; piety, 5, 8
plasma, 54
Plato, 17, 90; *Symposium*, 90; Cambridge Platonists, 59
Plotinus, 17
Poe, Edgar Allan, xvii, 28
Poland, 23
Polanyi, Michael, 57
Polhem, Christopher, 19, 29, 31, 32
Polhem, Emerentia, 29
Polhem, Maria, 29
politics, xxii, xxiv, 4, 75; *see also* Swedenborg, as statesman
Poltava, 19
Popular Mechanics, 29
Prague, 23
precognition, xvi, 82, 105, 108; *see also* clairvoyance; telepathy
Pribram, Karl, 43
proteins, 58
Protestant, 96
psyche, the, 64, 65
psychics, xvii, xxi, 12, 53, 55, 56, 72, 79, 102, 110
psychoanalysis, 72, 74
psychology, 2, 55, 60, 71, 77, 81, 87; psychological, xx, 2, 3, 10, 18, 40, 98, 112
Publilius Syrus, 18
Purgatory, 117
Pythagoras, 17

rational, rationality, 55, 56, 63, 65, 77, 79, 93, 94; rationalism, 75; modern Western, xiii; rationalist, xiii, xiv, 92
Ray of Creation, the, 46, 47
reality, xiv, xviii, 42, 59, 61, 89, 115, 117, 129, 133, 134; of soul, 38; spiritual/paranormal, 3, 98, 105, 112; TV, 74
rebirth, 3, 73
Redeemer, 89
religion, 2, 3, 5, 8, 81; religious, xix, 4, 50, 89
respiration, 9, 54; respiratory motion, 54; *see also* breath, control of

revelation, 85, 101, 130, 135
Revelation, 102
ribs, 103
Rilke, Rainer Maria, 125, 126; *Duino Elegies*, 125
Rimbaud, Arthur, 114; "Vowels," 114
Rittelmeyer, Friedrich, 96
Robsahm, Carl, 88, 89
Romantics, 79, 90, 114
Rome, 20, 23
Rosicrucians, xxii, 15, 22
Rough Guide, 115
Russians, 19

Sabbatai Zevi, 22; Sabbatian, 22
salvation, 8, 73; save, 81
Samadhi, 10
San Remo prison, xxii
Sartre, Jean-Paul, 121
Saturn, 49
schizophrenia, 11, 13
Schoenberg, Arnold, 123; *Jacob's Ladder*, 123
Schrödinger, Erwin, 57
Schuchard, Marsha Keith, xxi, xxii, 15, 21
Scripture, 1, 89, 92, 101, 102, 111; *see also* Bible
seer, 10, 107, 109
Self, the, 72, 73, 74
self-love, 5, 6, 26, 67, 79, 81, 116, 118
serotonin, 52
sex, sexual, 3, 13, 22, 23, 30, 31, 55, 66, 67, 73, 74, 75, 77, 115, 122; *see also* erotic
shamanism, 123; Indian, xix
Shaw, George Bernard, 57, 115, 116, 117, 119; *Man and Superman*, 115; Donna Ana, 116; John Tanner, 116, 117
Sheldrake, Rupert, 57, 58; morphic resonance, 57; morphogenetic fields, 58; *A New Science of Nature*, 57; *The Presence of the Past*, 57
sight, sense of, 12, 54, 94, 95, 96, 97, 98
signs, 112; Swedenborg's guiding sign or flame, 41; *see also* correspondences; symbols
sin, 2, 3; sinful, 12; sinner, 2, 92
Skåne, 19
Skara, 14
skull, the, 55
sleep, 87, 92, 94, 95, 97; asleep, 72, 85, 98; *see also* dreams; hypnagogia
smell, sense of, 11, 12, 13, 14, 76, 97; odors, 11, 91, 115; *see also* Jacobson's organ; pheromones
Socrates, 41; *daimon* of, 41
Södermalm, 106
solar system, the, 47; *see also* cosmos, the; sun, the; universe, the
soul, 9, 15, 38, 39, 40, 52, 53, 55, 56, 58, 59, 64, 65, 66, 67, 72, 73, 74, 78, 79, 82, 83, 110, 120, 121, 124
space, 41, 42, 122, 123, 133; inner, xviii; spaceless, 42; *see also* cosmos, the; universe, the

spiral, 45, 47, 49
spirit(ual) world, the, xvi, xviii, 6, 11, 12, 18, 30, 55, 97, 98, 101, 102, 107, 108, 110, 111, 112, 113, 118, 123, 125; *see also* world of spirits
spirit(s), xxi, 9, 11, 12, 41, 49, 59, 67, 83, 89, 92, 95, 97, 98, 103, 110, 112, 120, 123, 125; evil, 11, 86, 91, 94, 120; possession by, 91; *see also* dead, the
spiritual, xix, 2, 11, 23, 65, 66, 85, 89, 96, 111, 112, 115, 124; angels, 125, 127; crisis, 1, 13; experiences/investigations, xx, 96; growth/development, 2, 105; heaven, 124; paralysis, 93; reality/life/state, 3, 10, 66, 98; rebirth, 73; salvation, 73; scientist, 40, 92; sense/meaning, xx, 89; smell, 11; suffering, 8; things, 2, 89; thinker, xviii, 62; traditions, xix; writings, 17, 33
spiritualists, 109
spirituality, 3, 23, 51, 89
St. Paul, 109
Stanley, Michael, 53
stars, 46, 48, 49; novae, 49; pulsars, 49
Stein, Gertrude, 112
Steiner, George, xix
Steiner, Rudolf, xvii, 40, 58, 92, 96, 97, 98, 109, 110; and the Akashic Record, xvii, 96, 97
Stockholm, 4, 14, 32, 106, 107; Södermalm, 106
Strindberg, August, xvii
Stuarts, the, xxii
subjective, 60, 80, 95, 133; subjectivity, 80; subjectivization, 22; *see also* consciousness; experience
sun, the, 45, 46, 48, 49, 84, 111, 112, 123; *see also* solar system, the
supernatural, 38, 39, 83, 128; *see also* paranormal
superstition, xiii, xv, 61; superstitious, xiv, 105
Swedberg, Jesper, 4, 5, 6, 7, 8, 14, 16, 17, 18, 19, 29, 31, 37, 52
Sweden, xx, xxi, 4, 5, 18, 19, 20, 26, 28, 29, 30, 31, 32, 106
Swedenborg, Albrecht, 6
Swedenborg, Anna, 14
Swedenborg, Emanuel, ambition/recognition/desire for fame of, 1, 3, 16, 24, 26, 29, 67, 73; and Board of Mines, xx, xxi, 4, 21, 31, 32, 82, 92, 93; correspondences, 18, 55, 64, 111–14; Doctrine of Series and Degrees, 61–5, 124; and economics/currency reform, xx, 33, 37; and engineering/mechanics, xx, 24, 27, 28, 29, 31, 32; Grand Man, the, 46, 104, 124; health of, 20, 76, 86; as inventor, xx, xxi, 1, 26–7, 29; his paranormal/clairvoyant abilities, accounts of, xvi, 106–9; as poet, xxi, 16, 17, 23, 33, 89; sanity of, 12, 82, 87, 91–4, 98, 102; as scientist, xx, xxi, 1, 5, 9, 10, 11, 15, 16, 17, 18, 19, 21, 24, 25, 26,

31, 32, 33, 37, 38, 39, 40, 48, 50, 51, 52, 53, 59, 73, 75, 77, 78, 79, 86, 89, 103, 114; and Scripture interpretation/exegesis, xix, xx, xxi, xxiii, 1, 24, 26, 84, 89, 92, 101, 102, 111, 113; as secret agent, xxi; and sex/eroticism, 3, 22, 23, 30, 31, 51, 55, 66, 67, 73, 74, 75, 76, 77, 89; search for soul, 9, 38, 39, 40, 52–6, 58, 59, 64–7, 78, 79; his speech impediment, 16, 32, 104; spiritual crisis and doubt of, 1, 2, 3, 20, 23, 39, 49, 71, 81, 82, 84–7; as statesman, xx, xxi, 32–3, 92; as theologian, xvi, xxi, 16, 21, 46, 55, 64, 74; travels of, xx, xxi, xxiii, 1, 18–25, 31, 52, 71, 73, 82; university studies of, 14–17, 45; works of, *The Animal Kingdom*, 82; *Arcana Coelistia*, xviii, xix, 102, 111, 113, 114; *The Cerebrum*, 52; *Conjugial Love*, 7, 18, 30, 51, 103; *Daedalus Hyperboreus*, 24, 29, 31, 37; *The Economy of the Animal Kingdom*, 40, 52, 64, 78; *Heaven and Hell*, 18, 102, 125; *The Infinite*, 50, 78; *Journal of Dreams*, 2, 3, 12, 67, 71, 73, 74, 75, 77, 78, 79, 91, 105; *Philosopher's Notebook*, 24; *Philosophical and Mineralogical Works*, 38; *Principia*, 38, 42, 48, 50; *Spiritual Diary*, 1, 2, 7, 12, 41, 87, 91, 94, 125; *Word Explained*, 41; *Worlds in Space*, 49; *Worship and Love of God*, 33, 89;

Swedenborgians, xvi, xxiii, 21, 30
Symbolism, xvii, 113, 114
symbols, 41, 72, 112, 114, 126; symbolic, 72, 111; *see also* correspondences; signs
synaesthesia, 114
systems theory, 47

Tanner, John, 116, 117
tarot, xiv
teleology, 57
telepathy, 105, 108; *see also* clairvoyance; precognition
temptation, 66, 81; tempt, 26; tempter, 85, 86
Tesla, Nikola, 95
theologians, xxi, 122
theology, 4, 15, 16; Lutheran 17; theological, xvi, xxiii, 21, 33, 46, 55, 64, 74, 91, 103
Theosophical Society, London, 21
Thoth, 128; *see also* Hermes Trismegistus
time, xviii, 41, 45, 48, 122, 123, 133; timeless, 42, 123
Tipler, Frank, 49; anthropic cosmological principle, 49
Toksvig, Signe, 4, 5, 11, 30, 51, 96
Trollhättan, 32
Tulk, Charles Augustus, 30
Turkey, 19
Tuxen, General Christian, 96, 97

Ulrika Eleonora, Queen of Sweden, 32
unconscious, 74, 86

universe, the, xiv, 38, 42, 44, 46, 48, 49, 50, 63, 64, 104, 124, 126; *see also* cosmos, the; solar system, the; space
Upanishads, the, 85
Uppsala, 4, 15; university of, 5, 14, 15, 16, 17, 45

vagina dentata, 74, 75, 77
Van Dusen, Wilson, 41, 77, 78, 79, 86, 87, 98
van Helmont, François Mercure, 15; *Kabbala Denudata*, 15
Vaucanson, Jacques de, 28
vegetable world, 63
veins, 103
Vienna, 110
Vieussens, Raymond de, 52
vital body, 62
vitalist, 57, 59
vortex, 45; *see* also spiral

Wallace, Alfred Russel, 57
war, 32; warfare, 28; Swedish defeat to Russia at Poltava, 19
Watson, Lyall, 13, 14; *Jacobson's Organ*, 13
Weimar, 110
Wesley, John, 108
Westphalia, 23
Wilkinson, James John Garth, 30
Willis, Thomas, 52
Wolff, Christian, 71, 72
world of spirits, 21, 89, 98, 101, 117, 125, 130, 135; *see also* spirit world, the

Yeats, William Butler, xvi, 22
yogis, 10
Young Pretender, the, xxii

Zinzendorf, Count Nikolaus Ludwig von, 22, 23